THE
TOURISM DEVELOPMENT
H A N D B O O K

A Practical Approach to Planning and Marketing

Kerry Godfrey
and
Jackie Clarke

CONTINUUM

The Tower Building
11 York Road
London SE1 7NX

370 Lexington Avenue
New York
NY 10017-6503

www.continuumbooks.com

First published 2000. Reprinted 2000, 2002
British Library Cataloguing-in-Publication Data
A catalogue record for this book is available from the British Library.

ISBN 0-8264-5337-6 £ 23·65

Typeset by Sam Merrell, Bath
Printed by Martins the Printers Ltd, Berwick upon Tweed

Contents

Foreword

Tourism is one of the world's fastest-growing industries. International tourism, despite periodic upheavals, continues to expand on average at between 4 and 5 per cent annually, and by the year 2000 there are likely to be well over 650 million international visitor arrivals worldwide, quite apart from the much larger number travelling within their own countries. Despite fuel and airport taxes the real cost of travel continues to decrease. More and more people are on the move – whether on holiday, away for a short break, out for the day or on a business trip – and all this activity provides employment for millions, generates income for millions more, and results in satisfaction or frustration according to experience. But tourism is also (often rightly) blamed for damage to the environment and its impact on local cultures and ways of life. As more and more people travel, it becomes ever more important, therefore, that tourism should be properly planned for and managed, and much of this has to be done at local level.

Tourism is of course highly competitive. For those planning a holiday or short break, business visit or conference, the array of potential destinations has massively increased, with ever more exotic alternatives on offer. Standards are higher, travellers' expectations have increased and traditional holiday destinations can no longer rely on old loyalties.

The successful destination, as this book makes very clear, will be aware of its strengths and weaknesses, build on the former and seek to overcome the latter. Its strengths must be real and not just wishful thinking on the part of over-exuberant tourism officers. Such a destination will have compared itself with its competitors, but not simply sought to copy them. It will have developed its own unique character and decided what sort of a place its community wishes to be. It will have identified its target markets and geared both product and promotion to satisfy the needs of those markets. Its strategy will take account of the necessity to care for its environment and heritage, and, perhaps above all, it will go out of its way to be welcoming. This means winning the support of all sectors of the local industry and having the community on its side – each sharing in the planning process, agreeing the strategy, its goals and targets, and playing a part in its successful implementation. It may also mean setting limits on the scale or type of development permitted in the interests of long-term sustainability.

Those responsible for planning, developing and managing tourism destinations and who read and follow the advice set out so simply in these pages should be well on the way to a successful and sustainable future.

Stephen Mills, MA, FCA, FTS
Former Deputy Director (Development)
English Tourist Board

Introduction

Tourism development planning at the destination level is a step-by-step process of resource and market evaluation, action and review. Its broad purpose is to recognize gaps in the local product or market, identify project ideas to fill those gaps, and recommend actions to put those ideas in place. Often called the 'systems approach', it is driven by long-term goals, where the destination is developed systematically through small actions, each contributing to the end result, piece by piece.

However, tourism development is no economic panacea, and getting the most from the industry requires careful planning and management. In some areas, no matter what the capital injection, tourism may not work if ill-planned or mismanaged. In other areas there may be great local potential, and all that is needed is a little guidance on how to go about planning in a systematic and organized fashion. However, even where tourism does present a significant development opportunity, a destination may still fail if all the components of good development are not considered.

With these points in mind, this handbook has been written to assist anyone in the preparation of a tourism development strategy for a local destination area. Designed so it can be used in sequential order or dipped into at specific points, the book presents a discussion of the practical steps involved in the planning and marketing of tourism from a local or regional perspective.[1] The book is not a traditional or definitive what-to-do text of tourism development principles, nor is it necessarily concerned with the production of a formal tourism master plan. Rather it represents a systematic how-to or self-help guide which seeks to explain the many components, practical steps and activities involved in the preparation of a tourism development strategy (see Figure I.1).

The focus of the handbook is a checklist format, designed to encourage users to ask themselves the right questions in assessing the tourism potential of their area. While the steps and activities it contains are rooted in the theory of tourism planning and marketing, they are practice oriented and

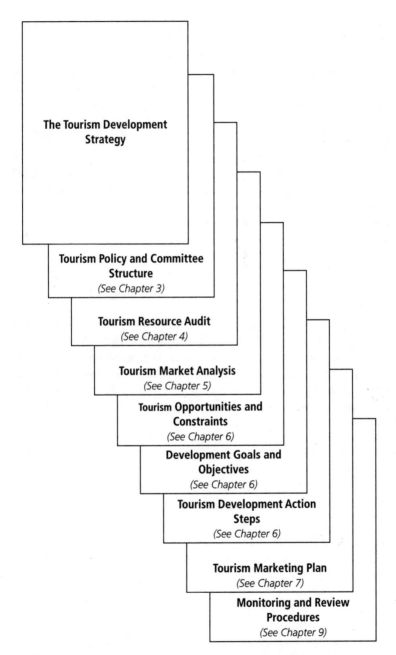

The Tourism Development
Strategy

**Tourism Policy and Committee
Structure**
(See Chapter 3)

Tourism Resource Audit
(See Chapter 4)

Tourism Market Analysis
(See Chapter 5)

**Tourism Opportunities and
Constraints**
(See Chapter 6)

**Development Goals and
Objectives**
(See Chapter 6)

**Tourism Development Action
Steps**
(See Chapter 6)

Tourism Marketing Plan
(See Chapter 7)

**Monitoring and Review
Procedures**
(See Chapter 9)

Figure I.1: Basic Components of a Tourism Development Strategy

applicable to a wide range of destination types based on community resources and involvement (e.g. heritage tourism, cultural tourism, rural tourism, island tourism, coastal tourism, event tourism, etc.).

The book is primarily designed as a quick point of reference for people who do not necessarily have the time or desire to wade through rather heavy academic or other general texts on tourism planning and marketing. It is intended as a professional *aide-mémoire* for those people already working in travel and tourism (planners, marketers and project managers in destination communities and tourist regions), and a refresher course manual for graduates and other people making a career change into the tourism sector. Its usefulness of course will be best measured by the ragged and well-worn copies used in the ongoing process of tourism development and management in destination areas.

K. B. Godfrey
J. R. Clarke
Oxford, UK

NOTE

1 The definition of tourism adopted in this handbook reflects the comprehensive definition used by the World Tourism Organization and includes both domestic and international tourists; package and independent travel; car, coach, train and plane travel; business, sports, VFR (visiting friends and relatives) and educational tourists; day-visitors (excursionists) and overnight visitors (tourists). It covers all aspects of tourist travel which can take place in a destination area.

CHAPTER ONE

What's all the fuss about?
Tourism development in context

INTRODUCTION

Tourism is big business. Internationally, it represents one of the world's largest economic industries. With nearly 600 million visitor arrivals (around the world) estimated by the millennium, some now claim tourism accounts for 1 in every 14 workers, and up to 12 per cent of global gross domestic product.[1] As personal living standards and disposable income continue to improve, with fewer restrictions on travel and with more convenient and cheaper transport, both the contribution from tourism to the world economy, and the overall number of tourists, are expected to grow.

Without a doubt, tourism is an increasingly important economic activity. However, as the industry has grown it has also become much more diverse and complicated than it was in the 1970s and 1980s. Traditional patterns of long holidays are being replaced with more frequent and shorter lengths of stay. Activities have modified, with greater interest in learning something new and individuality rather than in the simple mass standardization of products. Tourists are also placing greater emphasis and concern on environmental quality of destinations, value for money and better customer service.

With the beginning of a new millennium, virtually everyone from national governments to local communities seems to be jumping on the tourism bandwagon. Many new opportunities for travel and new destinations have been brought to the market as a result. However, not all have been, or will prove to be a success. For tourism to succeed today it must be sustainable economically, socially and environmentally. To be sustainable it must be carefully planned and managed, taking account of many different factors. Experience has shown that destinations which fail to protect their resources and provide a quality visitor experience are being overlooked in favour of those which do.

> *For tourism to succeed it must be sustainable ...*
> *to be sustainable, it must be carefully*
> *planned and managed*

WHAT IS TOURISM PLANNING?

Tourism planning generally takes place at three different levels: nationally, locally and of the individual attraction. At the national level, it involves the co-ordination and management of large tourist regions or the country as a whole, usually through the development of policy, national standards and institutions. At the **facility** or **site level**, it involves the planning, design and development of individual tourist attractions, services and facilities to serve tourist needs. Less common though equally important is the planning and management of **tourist destination areas**: the organization and development of visitor attractions and services in and around destination communities. This is known as the **community** or **destination level** of tourism planning, and is the focus of this book.

Until very recently, destination tourism planning was often a somewhat isolated or *ad hoc* procedure. Government and industry alike would under-take basic assessments of market demand, think of what could be done or developed to meet that demand, establish a programme of development in response to that demand, and then seek to promote it to potential visitors. Modern tourism, however, is very dynamic. Changes in what tourists want, when they travel, how they travel, and what they're willing to accept have made this relatively static and linear procedure of plan-then-develop highly obsolete and potentially dangerous in a commercial sense.

Many communities have now begun to realize they need to be more responsive and proactive in their approach to tourism. They are showing con-cern over what is actually developed, how it is promoted and the impacts this might produce with regard to economic, social *and* environmental factors. Tourism planning is now more than just developing new or better attrac-tions, increasing the number of visitors, or seeking to boost profits. Rather, it is all about promoting orderly development of the industry.

Today, destination planning involves setting goals and objectives for the industry, understanding present market conditions and trends, recognizing issues and possible constraints, creating opportunities, identifying altern-atives and recommending action. When done well, it should lead to the timely and better development of suitable projects and a superior tourism service. When done poorly, or not at all, then lower financial returns, less satisfied customers and a damaged resource base are often the result. The days when planning simply meant pushing tourism for the sake of development, through financial incentives and the unlimited exploitation of resources, are no longer viable.

> **Tourism planning is about promoting orderly development of the industry**

Planning and management are central to the long-term sustainability of tourism and must take place at all levels of activity. However, experience has shown that it is at the community or destination level that the real action takes place, and where the various impacts of tourism are most acute. After all, it is here where the jobs are created, the attractions exist and the tourists visit.

TOURISM AND THE COMMUNITY

Communities are a basic element of modern tourism. They are the focal point for the supply of accommodation, catering, information, transport facilities and services. Their local natural environment, buildings and institutions, their people, culture and history, all form core elements of what the tourists come to see. Whether as towns, villages or cities, every community has tourism at one level or another, and is affected by the growth and development of the industry.

Many of the problems associated with modern tourism are not necessarily the fault of tourists or tourism *per se*, but more the result of poor planning and a haphazard approach to development and management. Far too often destination areas have sought to promote and encourage tourism without any real thought given to the long-term consequence or potential negative impacts. Success was measured simply in terms of how many people a place could attract, and how much those visitors would spend in their area. Today, however, this is considered somewhat naïve and potentially counterproductive, as there are many other factors within and without the control of destinations which can affect profits and sustainability.

> **Destination communities are a basic element of modern tourism**

What many have seemingly failed to recognize or understand is that tourism is an agent of change. That is, wherever tourism development takes place, it can bring about a change in the way we use some resources to serve the tourist market. For example, when an old warehouse is redeveloped as a hotel, a redundant church turned into a visitor centre, holiday cottages built, or empty shops converted into tea shops, all of these mean a change of use. The facility may still exist, but the original function has been replaced by something new, and the resource has been altered. Tourism destination planning is about managing this change in a way that brings the greatest benefit to an area with minimal cost.

In many cases, the type and extent of change brought about by tourism is of no great concern and more often represents a benefit to the community. However, this is not always true. When shops selling goods to residents are replaced by those selling only souvenirs; when open space or playing fields are paved for visitor parking (without alternatives); or when tourist areas are cleaned up while local neighbourhoods are left untouched, then these changes may not be so good after all. Tourism destination planning must recognize that there are limits to this kind of change which is acceptable to a community, and reflect this in the goals and objectives of the plan itself. To do so, however, those responsible for planning tourism's development must fully understand and appreciate the impact tourism can have on local quality of life, and its effect on local natural and cultural resources.

> *Tourism planning must recognize that there are limits of change acceptable to a community*

UNDERSTANDING TOURISM IMPACTS

Tourism is a growth industry, offering communities of all shapes and sizes a unique development opportunity. However, not every community is suited to tourism, nor for that matter is tourism development necessarily appropriate for every community. Tourism impacts can be both good and bad, and the actual effect depends very much on the character of the area and local circumstance. On the plus side, tourism is widely recognized for creating and sustaining jobs, and bringing new money to an area. Visitor spending supports local business, speciality shops, restaurants and recreational facilities which might not otherwise survive. Tourism can also lead to the regeneration of redundant buildings, help with local conservation and environmental improvement, and be a key source of civic pride.

On the negative side tourism jobs are primarily in the service support sector, often low paid and part-time. The balance of local shops may shift away from convenience and everyday consumer goods to antiques, gifts and teashops. Increasing tourist activity can also lead to local congestion, litter, and wear and tear on local resources and infrastructure. Although tourism is undoubtedly important at a national level, particularly in terms foreign exchange and international trade, what it means for individual communities can be and often is quite different.

Destination tourism planning is about finding a balance between these costs and benefits in the best interest of tourism and the community. Tourism is no economic panacea, and economic development should never be the exclusive goal of the industry, particularly in a local setting. While tourism is often important to communities, driving its development only with regard to generating jobs and income tends to lose sight of the negative effects and does not adequately plan to minimize them. Due to the nature of its impacts, tourism should not form the core element of a local economy, but is better suited to play a supplementary role to help diversify economic activity.

> ***Tourism is no economic panacea, and is best suited as a supplement to a local economy***

Each destination needs to be sensitive to many factors which may affect its success. Like any other industry, tourism planning must build on a comprehensive understanding of its potential, to help maximize the industry's contribution to the well-being of a community and where possible eliminate the negative (see Chapter 2). However, community tourism is not a simple product or single business, but has many aspects including transport, accommodation, catering, attractions, information and hospitality. To be successful, destination communities need to establish leadership and co-ordination of all those active and interested in tourism.

DEVELOPING LEADERSHIP AND CO-OPERATION
While tourism is a very big industry on a global scale, at the local level it is also very small. That is, the vast majority of tourism companies are small or medium-sized operations, all offering a wide range of goods and services to the traveller in one form or another. This fragmentation in supply, however, can lead to variable quality in the local product, unnecessary competition, poor information flows and missed opportunities. While diversity is good, it can also create a weakness in the ability of communities to exploit tourism's full potential. With many small operators each seeking to maximize their own position, the wider interests of the whole industry are easily overlooked. To be sustainable, collective action is required.

However, tourism is not just the prerogative of the private sector. Some aspects of the industry (such as information and infrastructure) are often the direct responsibility of local government. In addition, many non-profit and voluntary groups may affect tourism through their own activities, such as conservation and preservation, or by running local festivals and community events. Therefore while the private sector may play a key role in tourism, it is not alone and should not act alone. Past evidence suggests that the best destination development plans are those created jointly by non-profit organizations, local government and the private sector. Success in local tourism flows from collaboration and complementarity, not internal competition and division. Organization and co-ordination are the key.

> ### Tourism development is not the prerogative of the private sector

Yet with many different players from both the public and private sectors, getting organized can be one of the first obstacles to overcome. Very often local groups, such as a chamber of commerce, hotel association or local government tourism department, have focused their tourism efforts on specific activities, such as promotions, but have rarely taken a more comprehensive view of development. Ideally, one group should take overall responsibility for managing local tourism. Some form of umbrella group is needed which draws representation from, and co-ordinates the activities of other local groups (see Chapter 3). Being organized puts the community in a better position to respond to changes in demand, improve information flows, enhance quality control, invest in the local product and develop human resources. Without an overall structure to which all groups can belong, contribute and interact, duplication of effort, reduced efficiency and lost opportunity tend to be the result.

It is not so surprising, however, that getting organized is just the beginning of the planning and development process. Generally speaking, the most successful tourism today is built on a clean physical environment and the positive expression of local culture and society. Tourists need something to see and have something to keep them occupied. They need a place to go to – a place which offers the chance to experience something completely different from their home environment. Otherwise why travel? Tourism planning is all about creating that place; building on the unique geography, history and cultural traditions that are evident in most communities. Understanding the extent and quality of these (and other) local resources represents the foundation of the destination area development plan.

UNDERSTANDING RESOURCES

Successful tourist destinations are those which offer the visitor something unique: they create a sense of place, an identity which is different from their competitors. Far too often communities with little previous experience of tourism growth simply look to their neighbours or other successful destinations when beginning a new development agenda. Unfortunately, the subsequent replication of too similar attractions in town after town tends to limit rather than encourage tourism success. The problem with this approach is that no two communities are ever exactly the same, either in terms of what they have to offer, or the visitors they can attract. Nor should they be. Even if Town A is good at tourism, this does not mean that Town B, with apparently very similar resources will have equal success just because it is near by. There may be and often are similarities, but there will also be differences and it is these differences which are so important to tourism.

> *No two communities are exactly the same ...*
> *nor should they wish to be*

The challenge facing many communities is deciding where to begin and how to determine what they have which may be attractive to visitors. The answer is usually a *Tourism Resource Audit*. The tourism resource audit involves a thorough assessment of a community's tourism supply: those features which can and do attract tourists to the community. This includes the analysis of what tourists come to see and do (attractions and activities), how they are served (hospitality and service), how they travel and get about (access and infrastructure) and how they are informed (information and interpretation) (see Chapter 4). They are designed to help destination communities identify what is special about them, but they also seek to determine what, if anything may be missing from the local product, and what needs improvement.

Tourism resource audits help destinations to identify linkages in supply, and opportunities which could be pursued to increase their attractiveness to potential visitors. Tourism development, however, is not just about building new facilities or attractions. Very often destination communities already have a number of the basic building blocks of tourism in place (attractions, services and hospitality), but they do not act together. In this setting, tourism development may be more concerned with the consolidation of tourism supply (the organization, packaging and presentation of resources already available), than of building new facilities or creating new attractions. In whatever situation, however, when properly carried out, tourism resource audits force communities to take an objective view of the local product (both good and bad points) and are the baseline from which all future development activity is measured.

> *Tourism resource audits are the baseline of future development activity*

Knowing what resources you have and their tourism quality is fundamental to destination planning. However, this is only half of the development equation. Success in tourism comes from being able to match what a place has to sell, or could potentially sell, with what visitors want and are willing to pay for. Just as it is important to know what resources you have available for tourism development, it is equally important to determine who your current and potential visitors are and what they have come to see or do.

UNDERSTANDING TOURISM MARKETS

People travel for any number of reasons. They may be seeking rest and relaxation, activity and adventure, or perhaps a combination of anything in between. Tourists come in all shapes and sizes, each with their own needs, wants and desires for their visit. As with the analysis of supply, not all tourism destinations will attract all types of tourists, nor are all types of tourists attracted to similar destinations. They may be young and on their own, or perhaps more mature and travelling as a group. They may be there on business, visiting friends and relatives, staying for a few days, or just passing through on their way to somewhere else. Understanding these and other reasons why people travel in general, and why they travel to any particular place is a key element in determining a community's tourism market potential.

Tourism Market Analysis, as with any other product, is a key step in assessing an area's development potential. After all, there is little value in tourism if potential visitors are not interested in the product on offer. Tourism market analysis involves a thorough review of a local destination's tourism demand: who are the current visitors, where do they come from and when, what do they want to see and do, and what services and facilities do they require (see Chapter 5). Communities also need to know what influenced tourists to visit them, how they travelled and how long they are staying. At the same time, they need to determine who does not visit, as well as those who could be encouraged to do so in the future. These latter groups are significant in helping to diversify the market and avoid overdependence on any one particular market segment.

> ### *Tourism market analysis is a key step in the tourism development process*

Understanding tourism markets is a core element in the tourism development process, and is vital if local destinations are to match their product (*tourism supply*) with potential visitors (*tourism demand*). When complete it should provide destinations with the necessary information to identify and select those groups of visitors (*target markets*) most appropriate to their resources in terms of generating the greatest benefit, with the minimal cost. Success in tourism, however, will not happen on its own, but is built on a systematic and rational process of planning, action and review. Once complete, data from the market analysis is combined with the results of the resource audit in the preparation of the community's tourism development strategy.

DEVELOPING A TOURISM STRATEGY

Tourism destination development, as in any other service or retail industry, should follow a plan of action or strategy. Based on the review of local supply and demand, the tourism development strategy makes it possible to plan for improvements in existing products, explore opportunities for expansion into new markets and establish long-term priorities for the local industry. As a framework for decision-making, the tourism strategy represents a guide to all future development activity. It identifies strengths and weaknesses in the local product, defines a series of goals and objectives to address these issues, and outlines a plan of action to achieve these goals. In addition, as tourism development is an ongoing and dynamic process, the strategy also considers the evaluation and review of actions to provide a future measure of the plan's success.

Defining goals and objectives for tourism represents the core of the development strategy. *Goals* are general ideals which a destination would hope to achieve through tourism development activity. They are continuous concepts which may never readily be measured, but provide the general framework for a more specific series of objectives to follow. They are likely to concern such aspects as improving visitor satisfaction, diversifying tourism markets, increasing tourism's contribution to the local economy, and enhancing the area's overall tourism potential. In contrast, *objectives*, are much more specific and relate to actual activity. They are meant to guide action which will help to accomplish development goals. As such they must be realistic, measurable and able to be accomplished within a given time frame. If, for example, the goal is to enhance the overall tourism potential of an area, one objective may be to determine what new attraction could be developed, while another could be to encourage the development of new bed-and-breakfast accommodation in the community. Both of these could help to enhance tourism potential by adding something new to attract and entertain, and provide more places to stay.

> *Realistic goals and objectives are at the core of successful tourism development*

If goals and objectives are the core of the strategy, then the *Action Plan* is the substance of its implementation. Having derived a series of goals and objectives, a set of specific recommendations are devised in detail which spell out just how the objectives will be achieved. The action plan represents a series of small-scale activities which are feasible to implement and have definite outcomes. If, for example, the objective is to encourage new bed-and-breakfast accommodation, the action plan may involve: (1) highlighting the need for further tourist accommodation in local media; (2) arranging a seminar for local people on operating bed-and-breakfast facilities; (3) offering advice on promotions and advertising for new accommodation businesses; (4) ensuring new providers are listed in the local accommodation guide (see Chapter 6).

Throughout the development process it is important to keep in mind just how different goals may be achieved. In so doing it is more than likely the strategy will be realistic in what it hopes to accomplish. Indeed, as the object of tourism planning is its implementation, goals and objectives need to be achievable within the context of local resources and market potential. However, successful tourism development does not simply happen following financial investments in new attractions and infrastructure, or the creation of new services or facilities. These may be necessary and very beneficial, but communities that do not have a clear and realistic plan to attract visitors, who will appreciate these efforts, spend money and tell others of their visit, are likely to struggle to reach their potential.

THE MARKETING PLAN

Although destination development may begin with new ideas and new initiatives, it is as much to do with attractions and services as it is about marketing and promotion. Throughout the planning and development process, communities need to be thinking about who they want to attract as tourists, and how they are going to encourage them to visit. For many communities this simply means information and advertising. However, tourism marketing is much more than just selling a place to potential visitors. It includes the uniqueness of what visitors come to see (*the product*), the relative cost of one place compared to another (*the price*), the 'distribution' or accessibility of the place to potential target markets, and the variety of methods used to inform and attract visitors (*the promotional mix*). Matching the product, price and place with potential visitors is at the core of tourism marketing. Although advertising and information services are significant and tend to dominate local tourism budgets, their emphasis alone will not necessarily ensure success.

> ***Tourism marketing is more than just 'selling' a destination***

To reinforce a previous point, many communities with limited experience of tourism tend to look to neighbouring destinations for inspiration. In marketing terms this usually means trying to copy popular and highly visible promotional activities. This may seem logical, because they appear effective in one location, but as no two communities are exactly the same, what may work for one may not reach the right market for another. There is no universal or guaranteed method of attracting visitors. People travel for many different reasons and not everyone is equally interested in tourism. Indeed, similar destinations may appeal to different types of visitors, and communities should not try to attract everyone. Experience has shown that those which try to be everything to everybody tend to be less successful than those with a more defined approach.

Each destination must work out for itself its most appropriate markets, and determine what is the best approach to attract these preferred target markets. Knowing what a community has to offer, its current visitor profile and where they come from is a key starting-point in the marketing plan. The analysis of supply and demand should give a community a good idea of where it currently stands in the travel marketplace. As a framework for attracting visitors, the marketing plan identifies potential market segments as the focus of promotional activity, determines the techniques to be employed, sets a theme or image to be portrayed and establishes a time frame for its execution (see Chapter 7). However, travel trends and markets change. What may prove effective today may be less so next year. Therefore, ongoing evaluation and review of marketing plans are also important to test their general effectiveness in reaching target markets, and allow for adjustments in methods and techniques where appropriate.

> *Each community needs to work out its*
> *own approach to marketing*

Many aspects of tourism, however, are different from the development and marketing of other forms of business, not least of which is the sale of an experience. The tourism product is not something we can touch or feel. We cannot take it home at the end of the day, we cannot try it out before we buy and we generally cannot take it back if we are not satisfied or feel it does not really meet our expectations. In short, tourism is a risky purchase. Getting people to travel is only one element of success. Getting them to stay longer, spend more money, come back again and then tell their friends are where the real benefits appear.

DEVELOPING CUSTOMER SERVICE

Tourism is a business of both attracting and servicing the needs of visitors. Unfortunately, many communities seem to put a lot of effort into the attracting, but let themselves down when it comes to service and hospitality. We all like to be treated well when we travel, and most tourists have increasing expectations for the quality of personal service they receive at destinations. A visitor-friendly attitude must prevail if the local industry is to become and remain successful. A local destination may have outstanding natural scenery, fascinating culture, first-class attractions and an excellent location, but if the quality of service is poor, this could all be for nothing. The lack of understanding or recognition of this aspect of tourism development can mean the difference between mediocrity and something really worth talking about.

Customer service and hospitality are a way of doing business, an attitude towards visitors which makes them feel welcome and appreciated as guests in the community. This is important, because a happy tourist is more likely to return, be more willing to stay longer, spend more money in shops and restaurants, and to give a positive report to friends and neighbours when they return home. On the other hand, rudeness, price gouging, poor quality and a general lack of hospitality are a sure way of damaging a community's tourism reputation and its industry. Destinations need to pay close attention to quality of service and customer care from the outset. As a part of the tourism resource audit, service quality and hospitality are examined, with training programmes in customer care developed where necessary for all those involved in tourism services (see Chapter 8).

> *Attention to detail and customer care are*
> *vital to successful tourism development*

Customer care and tourism awareness, however, do not simply end with people directly employed in a tourist business or facility. Visitor satisfaction is also affected by the quality of service and reception from other community services (police, banks, health services, shops, etc.) and the general public. Indeed, tourism, like no other industry, is affected by the reception and friendliness locals display towards visitors. Hostility, or even indifference from the local population can have a negative effect on satisfaction levels. It is important to show the whole community that it has a role to play in generating tourism benefits, as well at the potential problems, through some form of tourism awareness programme.

The benefits of tourism will come if the quality of the visitor experience is high, and fostering awareness and public support are really only the start. To remain successful, tourism development must not only be carefully planned and implemented, but it also needs to be managed. Tourism and its impacts are dynamic, and any development plan needs regular evaluation and review to ensure the benefits of tourism growth continue to outweigh the costs.

MEASURING SUCCESS

Tourism development is an ongoing process. It begins with resource and market assessment, but does not simply end with the plans for implementation. To do so would leave the plan indefensible in terms of meeting its goals and objectives. A critical element of any tourism development process is to measure what has been achieved against what it was designed to do in the first place. Monitoring and review are essential in managing tourism impacts, and in assessing how well different actions have addressed development objectives. It helps to identify problems before they get out of hand, adapt to a changing marketplace, and measure the response to specific initiatives. It is therefore essential that before development takes place, or is further encouraged, a system to monitor and evaluate the effectiveness of actions is set in place.

> *Monitoring tourism development is*
> *essential to managing impacts*

To be effective, monitoring and evaluation need to be undertaken on a regular and systematic basis, involving economic, social and environmental indicators of both supply and demand. From a supply point of view this typically involves the assessment of occupancy levels, attendance figures and transportation flows against predevelopment values. It also means scrutinizing the response of the general community to development and the effects tourism has had on local quality of life. From a demand perspective this usually means collecting data on visitor satisfaction, market origins and travel motivations to better focus activities and guide future revision of the development plan itself. It also helps to determine how effective the strategy has been in terms of matching supply with demand (see Chapter 9).

Tourism development, however, does not occur in isolation, and the decision to increase tourism should be based on an evaluation of its potential costs and benefits. With proper planning and management, it can form a positive and successful element of a local economy. Yet this takes time, knowledge and skills which may not all be readily available in every destination. Communities are responsible for managing their own industry, but local tourism officers sometimes find themselves more in the role of facilitator or catalyst in the development process, with outside help brought in to provide extra technical assistance, advice and research expertise.

GETTING EXTRA HELP

Tourism is an increasingly complicated and market-sensitive industry, with many different organizations, companies and individuals all seeking to influence destination choice. Depending on the nature of the local product, the stage in the planning process, or the personnel available, it may be necessary to seek professional help in the preparation of the development plan. Increasingly, the use of tourism consultants is seen as one way of bringing new skills, new ideas and innovation to a community project. However, they can also be costly, time-consuming and possibly ineffective if the task they are set is not clearly identified and prescribed. It is important to establish clearly the goals and objectives for tourism development, and the outputs expected from any project report. A good consultant appreciates a well-organized client, which usually means a better outcome for all concerned (see Chapter 10).

SUMMARY

Tourism planning at the destination level is a step-by-step process of evaluation, action and review. Its broad purpose being to recognize gaps, identify new ideas and take action to fill those gaps. It is driven by long-term goals but with short-term actions, each contributing to the final objective, one piece at a time. It involves ongoing monitoring and allowing for revision in response to changing circumstance in the marketplace. Past experience suggests, those communities which follow a more systematic and strategic approach to tourism development and marketing are more likely to achieve greater long-term benefits.

However, to succeed requires a sound knowledge of how tourism works, the many different people and groups involved, and the advantages and disadvantages which development could mean for an area. This book has been written with these points in mind. Each of the following chapters are designed to provide basic guidance on the key aspects of tourism development discussed in this opening chapter. They represent the basic building blocks which should systematically lead to more informed decisions, giving the development of tourism the critical evaluation it needs to succeed.

NOTE
1 World Travel and Tourism Council, 1992; World Tourism Organization.

CHAPTER TWO

The Good, the Bad and the Ugly
Understanding tourism impacts

INTRODUCTION

Most places develop tourism because of its economic potential: it creates jobs; brings in new money; is relatively clean; and has minimal start-up costs. In addition to these monetary benefits, it can also help conserve national heritage, protect the environment and contribute to an improvement in the quality of life and well-being of local communities.

However, tourism has a down-side, and like any other socio-economic activity, it carries with it costs as well as benefits. Tourism is seasonal by nature, and thus so are many of the jobs. It can lead to local inflation and profits can 'leak' away to external suppliers and proprietors. It can also put a strain on local infrastructure and services, enhance social problems, increase pollution and lead to overcrowding and traffic congestion in different environments.

Thus, like any other industry, the development of tourism requires a sound knowledge of both the opportunities and constraints it represents to a destination. If planners and managers are to develop and maintain a sustainable and successful tourism industry, they will need to be more aware of, and understand tourism's impacts. In doing so they should be in a better position to consider the trade-offs necessary to achieve this goal. This chapter examines some of the major costs and benefits of local destination tourism to help foster this understanding as an aid in the development decision process.

THE NATURE OF TOURISM IMPACTS

Tourism impacts come in many shapes and forms. These are often discussed in terms of the economy, social structure and physical environment of destination areas. Economic aspects concern issues of employment, balance of payments and foreign exchange; social structure relates to issues of culture, lifestyle and human interactions; the physical environment concerns issues of landscape and land-use in both built-up and natural settings. While each of these impacts rarely occur in isolation, for ease of measurement and review they are often separated into *economic*, *socio-cultural* and *environmental* categories when discussed.

Much early work on tourism impacts focused particularly on the economic benefits, to the virtual exclusion of any social or environmental cost/benefit recognition. This emphasis was not surprising, however, given the relative newness of tourism as a potential economic development activity. Studies and reports were commissioned by both government and industry to show that investing in tourism was not some daft idea, but that it would lead to serious economic growth and regeneration. It was not really in anyone's interest, at least from a development point of view, to look for a down-side to this new boom industry (which were difficult to measure anyway), and economic data was easier to identify and manipulate.

Two key reasons for encouraging tourism development have been the income and employment benefits created by visitor spending. This type of impact has generally been seen as positive and desirable in most destinations. Tourists buy goods and services from local shops and facilities, they eat out in restaurants, stay in hotels, attend theatres and visit attractions. Their spending contributes directly to the profitability and employment opportunities within these businesses, and generates tax revenues for the public sector. This is not the end of it, however, as direct spending on accommodation, food, entertainment and souvenirs are paid out in wages to employees and used to buy in additional supplies, which in turn helps foster employment and further economic activity in other sectors of the destination (see Figure 2.1).

This combination of direct (by tourists), indirect (e.g. resupply) and induced spending (e.g. use of wages) is often referred to as the *multiplier effect*. Each level of spending leads to further spending and the recirculation of the original 'tourist dollar' in a destination's economy. The effect of the multiplier has been likened to the property of a stone dropped into a pond. The initial impact making the largest splash, with the resulting ripples spreading throughout the destination area. However, the overall significance of the initial 'splash' and subsequent 'ripples' depends on a number of interrelated factors, including the economic structure of the destination area, the nature of visitor facilities, their ownership, levels of investment and the type of tourism demand.

However, the economic gains derived from tourism are seldom exclusive of social or environmental change. After the advent of mass travel in the 1960s, many people began to question the conventional wisdom of tourism as an unconditional benefit. At first the short-term economic gains were obvious. Yet unplanned and mismanaged tourism growth was beginning to lead to serious environmental pollution and social conflict. Physical erosion, health and safety issues, cultural exploitation and 'concrete jungles' were starting to destroy the very reasons for visiting a destination in the first place. Tourism was beginning to damage tourism.

Today, while the legacy of unplanned tourism remains, the emphasis on new development activity has seemingly changed (on paper at least), as many of the original economic claims have come unstuck or at the very least reassessed. Environmental and social issues are now seen to be much more significant in destinations, as many have begun to realize that tourism development involves much more than just jobs and income. Now the popular (albeit somewhat ambiguous) concept of *sustainable tourism* accepts that all tourism creates change in a destination. A planned approach is considered essential if the marginal benefits of tourism activity are to outweigh its marginal costs, so this change remains in a positive direction.

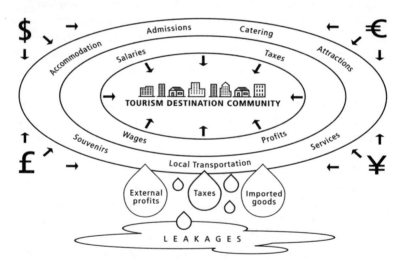

Figure 2.1: Tourism and the Local Destination

ECONOMIC CHANGE
The key elements of economic change associated with destination tourism include *employment, local income* and *economic diversification and regen-*

eration. Whenever tourism is discussed as a development option, it is these features which still tend to receive the most attention. This is usually because tourism is being used to help support or bolster a destination economy, and also because economic impacts are generally the easiest (in theory) to measure, are the most immediate to occur and reflect the general development initiative of the private sector. However, while tourism development undoubtedly supports employment, generates income and helps to diversify destination economies, not all economic impacts are necessarily positive. Indeed it would be somewhat irresponsible to pretend that these do not have associated costs. Each community will be affected in different ways, and while one place may be highly successful at tourism, another may receive very little benefit.

Employment

Most jobs associated with tourism tend to come in the form of direct service jobs in tourist-related facilities and attractions. These are primarily in hotels, attractions, restaurants, shops selling discretionary goods and travel firms. Further employment opportunities, however, arise in other sectors of the economy which service and supply the tourism sector, such as agriculture, fisheries, manufacturing and transport services.

Most direct tourism jobs, particularly in comparison to other industries, tend to be:

(+) at *entry-level*, requiring little or moderate skills and training;

(+) relatively simple and cheaper to create;

(+) are more labour- rather than capital-intensive (except when new facilities are required).

This tends to mean that tourism-related businesses are quicker to establish and require less initial financial input upfront compared to many other sectors of the economy. This is a particular benefit when creating new employment opportunities for young people, the unskilled and others who may be looking to supplement existing family income.

However, while tourists do spend money which directly supports local jobs, a number of these jobs tend to be:

(–) low-paid;

(–) seasonal;

(–) part-time;

(–) have limited career prospects, except in certain sectors, such as accommodation;

(–) have unsociable hours (especially in accommodation), with staff turnover relatively high compared to other economic activities.

In addition to these general features, in less developed areas new tourism enterprise often brings in outside expertise to manage facilities which further weakens the employment benefits to the destination.

Yet while the seasonality and nature of employment may not be perfect, these do tend to strengthen the viability of jobs in other sectors of the economy which supply tourism businesses, which in turn adds to general household income in the destination. Indeed, it is difficult to argue that tourism jobs do not represent a useful stepping-stone and strengthen the overall job market, helping those with little skill or experience into work, particularly where other employment opportunities are in short supply. This being said, the characteristics of tourism and the type of employment associated with it generally suit it to playing a supporting, rather than dominant role in a local economy.

Income

Visitor spending not only affects wages and employment opportunities, but generates income for both the public and private sector:

(+) tourist enterprises, like all local businesses, pay taxes to the government, and as tourism expands so too do these tax revenues;

(+) parking and admission fees collected from public sector facilities also bring in further general revenue resulting from tourism;

(+) if a local 'bed tax' or other form of 'tourist tax' is collected, this can represent further tourism revenue to a destination.

Often these additional funds can be used for the maintenance of publicly owned monuments and facilities, and contribute to future promotional and development activity of the destination.

However, the size and diversity of the local economic area determines the real value of tourism for a destination. Total visitor spending is meaningless on its own as it does not show what proportion of that spend actually stays in the local economy, after costs for imports have been deducted:

(−) virtually all local destinations have to import some goods and services to provide for and satisfy their visitors' needs and demands (i.e. food imports, souvenirs, secondary supplies).

The cost of imports cannot be included in calculating tourism impacts, as this does not give a true indication of the overall net benefit of tourism activity. The greater the economic diversification of the destination area, the less leakage there will be in terms of import costs. Indeed, the more local suppliers and services are used for all aspects of the industry, the greater the local economic benefit will be.

Economic Diversification and Regeneration

Relying on just one industry has proven to be problematic for many communities, particularly when that industry has gone into decline. Tourism is recognized as one industry which can help overcome the difficulties associated with the incumbent economic decline in these places, because:

(+) towns and cities are 'natural' destinations for visitors;

(+) tourism is often complementary to its other functions as a service centre, meeting point and seat of government;

(+) the tourism labour force is essentially in place;

(+) tourism is relatively clean, particularly compared to more traditional manufacturing and extractive industries.

As such, tourism tends to make a very attractive option in terms of local economic diversification and regeneration. However, as tourism activity grows, it tends to place demands on what are often limited land and labour resources. One consequence of this is local inflation, where:

(−) land prices may be forced up;

(–) wage demands may increase;

(–) physical space becomes a premium.

Increased property values may be good in one sense, however, they also lead to higher property taxes which some residents can ill-afford. This can lead to a change in the population structure, with fewer young people, and a non-resident community (holiday homes, etc.).

In terms of labour supply, fewer workers and increased tourism jobs can lead to firms competing through pay to get sufficient staff to service their tourism operations, which can affect viability. In some cases tourism can also lead to a local monoculture where:

(–) tourist-related shops can be more profitable and others traditionally supplying local needs are crowded out.

This is particularly evident in smaller centres where convenience goods may be replaced with antique dealers, art galleries, speciality clothes shops and tea rooms. While these facilities may add to the variety of local business, five novelty stores but no grocer may be undesirable. In addition, if these shops and facilities close down for the off-season, this can create a deserted appearance in some town centres. While tourist spending undoubtedly supports a wider range of goods and services than what might normally be feasible, these are sometimes of little use to local residents. A sense of proportion and balance should be maintained.

Finally, the development of tourism is much more than simply trying to attract visitors to an area. While economic regeneration and diversification is generally good, it needs careful planning and management to avoid negative impacts. Planning and management, however, are not free of costs. The proper development of tourism requires formal administration, survey research to underpin marketing activity, and impact studies to ensure development is appropriate to the area:

(–) planning and management have operational costs, and sometimes consultancy fees associated with them.

In addition, the added demands on local services by visitors need to be considered. Public safety, refuse collection, parking and open space are all influenced by tourist use. However, these costs should be recovered when tourists visit the area and spend their money in shops, attractions and other services.

The economic impact of tourism is not a simple derivative of total visitor spending, but is affected by a number of different factors. While each has significance at different levels of activity, it is the combined effect which really determines the overall outcome of tourism as an economic cost or benefit to a destination area. Each destination needs to understand those factors that are most relevant to it, to determine the nature and extent of their local impacts, and decide for themselves whether or not increased tourism development will be appropriate for them.

SOCIO-CULTURAL CHANGE

The key aspects of socio-cultural change associated with tourism destination development relate to local *quality of life* and *sense of place*. Social impacts differ from economic issues for obvious reasons, but also because they tend to have a more personal interpretation, take longer to appear and are much more difficult to measure. Socio-cultural change can be both real and perceived, and often tourism is but one of many factors which can be linked to this change. Social impacts develop through straightforward direct interpersonal encounters, or result from indirect or secondary association. However, whether real or perceived, direct or indirect, they are all equally important to understand, because it is often the social encounter (particularly if it is negative) which leaves one of the more lasting impressions on a destination and its visitors.

Quality of Life

Tourist spending in destinations often helps to support local facilities and services which are also used by the resident community. Often it is the additional income earned from tourism which helps keep some shops and services in business, which in turn:

(+) affects personal income;

(+) helps to improve living standards for those more directly involved in the industry;

(+) can make the difference between a business closing down in the winter or staying open throughout the year;

(+) supports the diversity of restaurants, theatre and other cultural entertainment;

(+) influence the assortment of goods for sale in many local shops that would not be available in the same amount if tourism did not exist to support them.

Tourist spending can also help a destination improve its facilities through tourist revenues. Visitor spending contributes to community income through taxes and admission fees, which in turn can be used to provide an enhanced local environment, where:

(+) park areas are often improved, street furniture and design criteria introduced;

(+) greater care and attention placed on overall environmental quality;

(+) new opportunities for recreation and other leisure pursuits which might not otherwise be realized without the additional or initial patronage generated from visitors to the area.

All of these aspects tend to enhance the local quality of life, by providing further opportunity and choice which might not otherwise exist, at least at the equivalent level or complexity.

Travel can also be personally rewarding as it can expose people to other cultures and language, expand personal horizons and enhance one's understanding of society. However, not everyone loves a tourist. Like anyone else, tourists can be loud and obnoxious, carefree in their attitude, overly demanding, damage the environment or be inconsiderate of property. They can lead to:

(–) increased traffic congestion;

(–) crowding of public places;

(–) longer queues in local shops and facilities.

Although obviously not life threatening, these all represent points of potential irritation, affecting quality of life, which can be further aggravated by seasonal strain. Crime may also increase, not necessarily caused by visitors, but by others preying on their unfamiliarity with an area and their leisured, albeit temporary, lifestyle. This can happen with:

(–) local shops overcharging;

(–) petty theft from cars and accommodation;

(–) pickpockets;

(–) or the more serious personal assault.

These social problems can further affect local quality of life, in particular when crimes spill over into the resident community, and if the image of a local destination declines with consequent fewer numbers and fewer services.

Large numbers of foreign visitors, with their different social habits, are seen by some to be a threat to local traditions, bringing unwanted change:

(–) resentment and in the extreme, xenophobia can develop (see Figure 2.2).

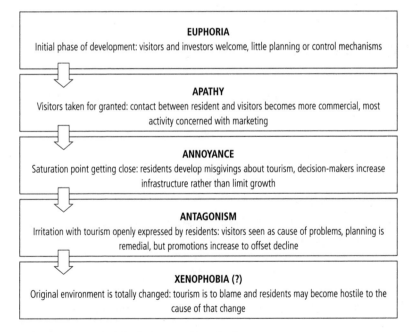

Figure 2.2: Modified Tourism 'Irridex' (after Doxey, 1976)

This model implies that as tourist numbers increase, they put pressure on the normal way of life for destination residents. It suggests the response of residents in different destinations will vary and change through time in a relatively predictable pattern of increasing irritation.

However, this is not always the case. Indeed the socio-cultural impact of tourism is often very different for different groups or individuals in a destination. Some will be very much in favour of tourism, while others may be negative (see Figure 2.3). This attitude is usually determined by a person's level of involvement or association with tourism activity in the destination area. Whatever the case, it is important to remember, that most people have or will at some point in time be a visitor themselves, either in other parts of their own country or overseas. Acknowledging our own actions and behaviour is relevant to understanding the socio-cultural implications of visitors elsewhere.

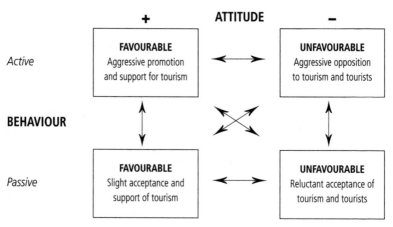

Figure 2.3: Personal Attitudes Towards Tourism
(source: Bjorklund and Philbruck, 1974, in Ryan, 1991)

Sense of Place
Tourists are often attracted to features of a destination which its residents may take for granted. Tourism can play a role in:

(+) revitalizing local culture and traditions;

(+) establishing or enhancing a sense of pride in local heritage;

(+) enriching local understanding and interest in history and culture.

Each of these can further help to strengthen civic pride and a sense of community. This is particularly important culturally and economically as it can help a community focus on a direction for future development and growth. In addition, what may attract tourists, such as recreation and leisure opportunities, a clean environment, local friendliness and sense of place, can also:

(+) influence industries and businesses to relocate or expand in the area.

Tourism can also lead to the preservation of culture, with past traditions reinvigorated. It often creates an audience for local arts and therefore:

(+) celebrations and festivals can become tourist attractions;

(+) crafts, folklore, dance and music can be given a new lease of life when they are seen to be of interest to visitors.

All of this can help improve the image of a community to the outside world, which when experienced by the visitor tends to encourage them to stay longer, spend more, return again and recommend the destination to others. This can further lead to a more positive outlook on tourism, particularly when it can be seen that cultural preservation brings an economic benefit to the destination.

However, while travel does, in most cases, help to widen a person's perspective and understanding, it can also lead to the commercialization of local culture and tradition. Many aspects of Western culture have become universal, and one consequence of this has been the development of tourism which neglects a destination's sense of place, where:

(–) festivals, activities and traditions which were perhaps core elements of a community may be transformed to better suit a growing tourist market;

(–) once authentic events may be restaged to make them more attractive;

(–) crafts may be modified and mass produced to make them more saleable and other features of culture broken down and packaged in a fashion attractive to the foreign visitor.

This has lead to a similarity in destinations, where a once distinguishing feature has been modified, becoming just like any other and widely available in the ubiquitous tourism marketplace.

Tourism can both improve as well as detract from the socio-cultural fabric of a destination. If problems are left to develop of their own accord, then the negative consequence may soon outweigh the benefits originally experienced. This can lead to a poor visitor experience, social agitation and possibly serious market decline. It is in everyone's interest to ensure that the development of tourism seeks to maintain a destination's unique identity and sense of place, for its residents as well as the visitors.

ENVIRONMENTAL CHANGE

The key elements of environmental change connected with tourism development primarily focus on aspects of *land and landscape* in the *built* and *natural environment*. These physical impacts tend to be the most visually apparent, because the development of tourism, like any other development activity, will change the physical location to some extent, wherever it exists. These physical impacts also tend to be the most emotive, as tourism can both protect and destroy the environment of a destination area. This issue is of particular importance because the destination's environment in all its forms is often the key reason for initial visitor interest in an area. If too much change occurs in any direction, the very reason for tourism development may be removed.

The Built Environment

Tourism has in many places provided both the means and justification for the conservation of our built or man-made heritage. Tourist interest in different aspects of culture has helped:

(**+**) to stimulate funds for, and the practice of, conservation and rehabilitation of historic buildings, sites and monuments all over the world;

(**+**) re-establish and present individual buildings and places of important events to reflect their former significance;

(**+**) encourage the regeneration, redevelopment and landscaping of town and city districts which no longer serve their original functions, having become derelict or rundown;

(**+**) the renovation of many redundant industrial and commercial sites into new shops and services, visitor attractions, hotels, apartments and exhibition space which would not likely exist if it were not for the tourist interest;

(+) lead to a renewed interest in transport systems and infrastructure from an earlier era, for example, steam railways, trams and riverboats, both as an attraction in themselves and as an actual means of transport;

(+) the creation of 'development control' policies and legislation, designed to provide a more active approach to maintaining environmental quality when new tourism development takes place.

Unfortunately these have generally followed significant damage caused by unplanned development of the industry and the significant influx of visitors. Although tourism has served to enhance our appreciation of nature and heritage, it has also led to increased pressure on these resources. The lack of planning or a strategic approach to the development of tourism has caused:

(–) problems of architectural pollution, where new buildings are somewhat at odds with the original character of an area;

(–) the creation of 'strip' or 'ribbon development' and urban sprawl particularly on the approach or access to destination areas;

(–) the straining of local service infrastructure, causing breakdowns in the supply of fresh water, sewerage systems and electricity;

(–) traffic congestion and parking problems leading to local aggravation, noise and environmental damage.

Many towns and cities have generally established some form of balance between human activity and their environment, but the haphazard development of tourism and the subsequent arrival of visitors has often affected this balance, causing a number of local problems. This is particularly true in heritage settings. Towns and cities originally designed and built before the motor car, with narrow streets and lanes, are particularly vulnerable to the modern mass transit of visitors. While the impact of individual tourists is rarely catastrophic on their own, the cumulative effect of many thousands over time is when the damage becomes most evident, with:

(–) wear and tear of stone fabric, worn down by the continual abrasion of tourist feet;

(–) fumes from tourist vehicles and Its effect on building façades;

(–) compaction of roadways and implications for underground sewers;

(–) structural damage caused by traffic vibration;

(–) graffiti and vandalism.

All of these issues need to be considered in the planning of tourism in heritage destinations. Without greater care and attention paid to these longer-term impacts, irreplaceable elements of cultural heritage may be damaged beyond reasonable repair.

The Natural Environment

A key feature of the latter part of the twentieth century, predominantly in Western society at least, has been the move towards an urban culture. This shift in living patterns, coupled with better mobility and greater leisure time has placed a renewed interest on the natural environment outside the urban form, both nationally and internationally, as a place for recreation and leisure. Increased demand and the consequent flow of visitor traffic to the rural hinterland, mountains and coast in many countries has increased pressure on these resources. At the same time, it has served to highlight the importance of environmental conservation if we are to continue to enjoy these places in the future.

Some of the more positive physical impacts of tourism in natural settings have been:

(+) the creation of park areas and renewed attention on the importance of wildlife and biological preservation;

(+) the 'sun, sand and sea' factors of tourism have highlighted concerns over ozone depletion and global warming and what this could mean for the place as well as the visitor;

(+) the depletion and contamination of water resources at sea and inland has also helped draw further attention to the need for better environmental stewardship and planning for all types of development activity, not just tourism.

However, while problems with tourism's impact has engendered greater

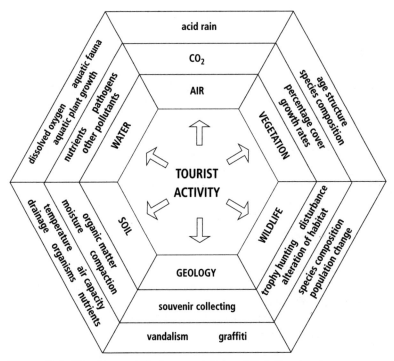

Figure 2.4: Tourism and Environment Impact Relationships
(adapted from Wall and Wright, 1977, found in Mathieson and Wall, 1982)

concern for the environment, it has also created a new demand for these natural places, which might not otherwise exist, particularly for those areas most readily accessible. More and more people travel to places highlighted for their scenic beauty or unique natural setting, leading to even greater environmental destruction. To meet growing demand, new roads are built or access improved, hotels are developed, with even more areas opened up to absorb the growing numbers (see Figure 2.4). The effect has been:

(–) the loss of vegetation for car-parks and other visitor facilities;

(–) trampling of plants and reduction in local biodiversity;

(–) the compaction and erosion of the soil;

(–) the general spread of garbage and litter.

Water quality has also been affected by:

(–) the reduction in water tables for consumption;

(–) pollution from increased run-off;

(–) the dumping of untreated sewage in lakes, rivers and the sea.

Finally, wildlife has also been affected by:

(–) disruption of predator–prey relationships and breeding patterns;

(–) loss of natural habitat to development;

(–) direct loss of wildlife populations through trophy and souvenir hunting and the trade in exotic species.

However, one positive outcome of these negative physical impacts has been the growth of interest in more environmentally sensitive and responsible forms of travel and tourist activity. *Green tourism* and *alternative forms of tourism* have been proposed by some as a key response to environmental degradation caused by the industry, with:

(+) low impact, unspoilt and environmentally friendly labels becoming commonplace both in new product features and destination policy;

(+) many travel firms are now promoting themselves as having '*green credentials*' and expressing a keen interest in conservation.

However, similar to the creation of development control policies in the built environment, much of this response has been superficial:

(–) with little more than platitudes to the broader concept of sustainability, after the damage has been done.

As with any kind of development, tourism will create change which may be inappropriate, obtrusive and cause problems if it does not reflect the sensitivities of the site or destination area. Careful planning and management of the industry are fundamental to mitigating tourism's environmental concerns.

FACTORS AFFECTING CHANGE

Tourism is a complex mixture of business and social activities, and its impacts do not necessarily happen to the same extent, at the same rate or are of equal importance in all locations. Indeed, what may be the impact of tourism in one place will not necessarily occur in another, even if it has similar features and is only just a few miles down the road. This means there is no simple cause-and-effect relationship which exists between a tourist destination and its visitors for all places or at all times. This is because the nature of tourism impacts are destination specific. Indeed, they are influenced by:

♦ local morphology (including political, social and economic structures of the destination;

♦ local ecology and environmental quality;

♦ the type of tourism activity and number of visitors involved;

♦ the difference in social attributes between residents and visitors;

♦ the nature of the interaction which takes place between them.

All of these factors are key elements of either *tourism supply* (essentially attributes of the destination) or *tourism demand* (the visitors). It is the match between supply and demand which effectively determines the ability of a destination to absorb tourism positively within its local environment and socio-economic structure.

Tourism Supply
Key elements of tourism supply in destination areas relate to the socio-economic structure of the destination, the nature of facilities and environment, ownership and aspects of investment. None of these features acts in isolation, but tend to influence each other, and it is how they interrelate which establishes the overall impact of tourism in a destination area.

Socio-economic Structure: The economic gains derived from tourism are directly related to the size, structure and diversity of the destination's economy. While total visitor spend is important as this partly determines economic impact, what they actually buy or spend their money on is more important. This is because:

♦ if the needs and demands of visitors cannot be met from local resources, then these will have to be imported.

For the purposes of destination impact analysis:

♦ imports are essentially anything and everything connected with tourism not produced and/or supplied from within the destination's own economic area (i.e. supplied or produced regionally, nationally or internationally).

As with all forms of imports, these have to be paid for, which means the amount of visitor spending associated with these imports leaves the local economy, and the level of positive impact is reduced.

Paying for imported goods and services in tourism is referred to as leakage. The greater the diversity of a receiving economy generally means it is more able to meet these needs without resorting to imports and so a lower level of leakage. Thus the larger and more developed the destination economy, the better able it is to supply the tourism industry from its own resources and the greater the economic impact:

♦ the level of economic leakage tends to increase as the size and diversity of the receiving economy gets smaller, and vice versa.

In this sense cities tend to get a better return from tourism than towns, and towns will gain more than villages, and so on. More remote and rural areas will generally have to import more goods and services to meet increasing demand and thus tend to have higher levels of economic leakage.

> *Economic leakage tends to decrease as the size and diversity of the destination gets larger*

Ownership: The economic benefits of tourism are also directly affected by the extent of local ownership;

♦ any local facility or attraction which is owned by 'foreign' (i.e. non-local) companies or individuals tends to have a smaller impact per customer than those owned and operated by persons drawn from the local resident community.

For example, in terms of accommodation, small hotels, guest-houses and bed-and-breakfast services, if locally owned and operated, tend to have a greater local economic impact, per visitor, than larger foreign-owned hotels. While the large hotel may hold more visitors overall, the majority of direct profits will most likely leave the local economy because they remit to the individual or parent company involved. This is also true for all shops, facilities and attractions in the destination:

◆ notwithstanding the obvious benefits of local employment opportunities and other benefits, in all situations, ownership has a significant influence on where most of the profits will flow and hence the impact on the destination economy.

This issue of ownership may also affect the supply of resources used by the facility and its personnel. It is possible that foreign-owned facilities, which tend to form part of a larger company, or have a head office elsewhere, will get a better economy of scale in terms of the purchase of supplies, by securing their resources from a national or central supplier:

◆ the result of external resourcing has the effect of reducing the overall impact on the destination.

Similarly, a foreign-owned facility may also use labour and management staff not drawn from the destination's labour pool, but brought in from other locations:

◆ wages paid out to these non-locals will also tend to leak out of the destination economy as they remit their earnings to home savings and investments.

> *A destination's economic benefits are directly related to the level of local ownership of tourism operations*

Investment: Tourists increasingly seek and demand better value for their money. They are looking for higher quality from tourism suppliers, but not necessarily at a higher price. Quality improvement, both in terms of structure and service, requires investment. Another key aspect of tourism supply concerns the level and type of investment made by both government and industry in developing tourism:

◆ investment in new facilities and infrastructure, upgrading and adapting older attractions, in education and training and in time and effort.

All of these cost money, which will have to be provided by both the public and private sector:

♦ public investment is usually made in terms of service infrastructure, transport networks and local amenities.

Generally, these are made to improve the basic foundations for tourism, and the incentive for private sector development. If this is drawn from local capital resources, then this may represent not only a direct cost to the local economy, but also an opportunity cost, as the funds may have been used for other development opportunities which are forgone in favour of the tourism investment. If, however, the investment funds are drawn from regional, national or international sources, then the direct and opportunity costs are significantly reduced, if not eliminated:

♦ private capital investment, on the other hand, generally relates to actual visitor attractions, facilities and other revenue-generating activities.

The private sector is unlikely to invest if there are problems with accessibility or a lack of other basic infrastructure which would make it difficult for visitors to get to the destination. Both public and private investment are usually necessary, especially if much private sector capital is to find its way into tourism investment opportunities in destination areas. However, the public sector is also sometimes reluctant to invest if it cannot see a direct benefit to the community. This is particularly true where local public funds for investment are limited, or where there is greater demand or need for other types of development. In this case external sources of finance may be the result.

Generally, the smaller the economic area in question the greater the likelihood of external finance. As with forms of ownership, however, external sources of private sector investment generally relate to higher levels of leakage relating to interest on the capital borrowed, and thus a smaller return to the local destination economy.

Nature of Facilities: Just as the structure of the economy is important to economic gain, so too is the nature of the facilities available in a destination. While much of tourism is travelling to see other places, one very popular activity for many visitors involves a certain amount of shopping. Some only buy one or two small souvenirs, while others may have saved specifically to look for a more significant memento of their visit:

♦ when there are limited opportunities for visitors to spend their 'holiday money' then the economic benefit of tourism tends to be limited as well;

♦ similarly, the greater the diversity of attractions and facilities on offer in a destination, the greater the opportunity to derive income from visitors through admissions fees and charges.

> *If opportunities to spend 'holiday money' are minimal, the economic benefits of tourism will be seriously limited*

It may be overstating the obvious, but if visitors have no place to spend their money, the economic benefits of tourism to a destination will be seriously restricted. Not surprising then, natural, wilderness and rural settings tend to achieve lower returns from tourism than more urbanized areas, because the level and diversity of spending opportunities tends to be less. However, even in towns and cities, economic impact can be significantly restricted if there are large numbers of visitors but minimal opportunities in which to shop for discretionary goods. This is particularly true of destinations which generally have large day-visitor markets but few types of overnight-stay tourists.

As with the issues of ownership and investment, locally owned and operated shops, facilities and accommodation will bring a greater return to the destination than national or foreign-owned chain stores and attractions. If these shops and facilities are supplied with locally produced goods, then a greater proportion of visitor spending will remain in the destination. Local employment created by all types of facilities are also a benefit. Whatever the case, the more opportunities there are in a destination where a visitor can spend their money, such as on accommodation, catering, attractions and services, the greater the economic impact will tend to be.

Nature of Destination: Many aspects of tourism supply tend to focus on the economy, but the physical and cultural environment are also core aspects which influence the level and direction of tourism-induced change. In terms of ecology and environmental quality, the physical environment of the destination is an important factor:

♦ more built-up areas, in towns and cities, will generally be better able to absorb visitors without significant environmental degradation;

♦ in contrast, more ecologically sensitive destinations, such as rural areas, mountains and lakes, tend to be less resilient to visitor use and more susceptible to environmental damage.

> **Each destination is different and will respond differently to the development of tourism**

Clearly each ecosystem is different and some can withstand significant visitor use without showing signs of strain, while others may show a major change with only minimal visitor contact.

In terms of socio-cultural impacts the nature of the destination is also a significant factor:

♦ again, towns and cities tend better to absorb the tourist function without causing significant social disruption.

Urban destinations tend to be more culturally and socially diverse. As a result they are more dynamic in dealing with the complexities of tourism demand. In contrast, more remote, rural and small-scale destinations tend to be far more homogeneous in their social and cultural structure and respond or react more strongly or tend to be more sensitive to socio-cultural change. Socio-cultural impacts are more pronounced and significant where the degree of similarity between the resident population and the visitors is minimal:

♦ the greater the difference in culture, social status, language, wealth, religion and values, the greater the tendency for socio-cultural impacts to emerge.

Tourism Demand

Facility ownership, economic structure, investment and the nature of tourist facilities are all elements of tourism supply. However, these factors will not alone determine the impact of tourism. They need visitors (tourism demand) to complete the supply and demand function. The central aspects of demand which most affect tourism change include the type of tourist (e.g. individual or mass), where they come from, the purpose of their visit and how long they stay in the destination.

Tourist Type: Clearly the total volume of tourists visiting a destination is important, as this will affect the overall level of spending and economic benefit. However, there are many different categories of tourist and tourism, and not all have the same effect. Some types of tourists spend more per person per day than others, which is generally related to their own socio-demographic characteristics and form of travel:

♦ the type of tourist, their individual spending power and the products actually purchased can be more relevant than total numbers.

On the whole, the more individual or independent tourist will have the greater economic impact per person than the mass or large groups of visitors. Individuals or small groups are more likely to make their own arrangements, stay in a variety of accommodation, eat out in a diversity of restaurants and visit attractions and facilities according to their own schedule. They are also more likely to pay for tourist services and accommodation directly in the destination area, apart from travel to and from the destination.

In contrast, at the other extreme, mass or large groups of visitors tend to travel in pre-arranged groups. Very often these 'all-inclusive tours have virtually everything decided and paid for in advance of travel. Catering, accommodation, entrance fees and activities are usually all packaged prior to the actual visit. In addition, as schedules and thus timing can be critical to the organized group so the opportunity or ability for these visitors to spend money locally can be minimized, at least outside the pre-arranged facilities. Although a broad generalization:

♦ small groups of independent, higher-spending visitors can be more beneficial than large organized groups of low-spending visitors despite the absolute numbers.

In terms of social issues, the type of tourism demand is one of the key factors in determining the level of impact tourists will have on a resident population:

♦ the ratio of residents to visitors, and the degree of actual contact between the two is often seen as a central factor in the attitudes displayed towards tourism and tourists in destination areas.

> ### *Not all tourists will have the same impact in every destination*

In the main the more visitors, the greater the possibility for interaction and impact. However, while large groups of visitors cannot help occupying space in the destination and potentially displace local people from some areas, this may not cause significant socio-cultural change. On the other hand crowding of public space, filling public transport, or contributing to general congestion in town centres, shops and services, may cause a certain degree of aggravation and intolerance. In contrast, small groups will not have the same physical presence, but their impact may be more acute, because they may develop a more personal contact with the destination and its population.

In terms of environmental issues (and leaving aside behavioural characteristics), smaller groups of visitors will have less of an impact than large groups at any one point in time. Smaller groups can be more readily accommodated without many extra facilities and services. However, small groups and individuals tend to be more adventurous and may explore an environment more thoroughly than larger groups which confine themselves to the more established elements of a destination:

♦ over time the individual's impact may become more significant through the cumulative effect of several independent visitors if there is not enough time for a particular environmental setting to recover from previous use.

Point of Origin: Where a visitor comes from will also significantly affect the level of tourism impact. Overseas or international tourists are more likely to spend more per day than domestic or intra-national tourists, primarily because of the cost of accommodation and travel. However, this distinction becomes less significant in terms of the impact in actual destination areas below the national or regional economic level:

♦ there may be little difference in the actual spending patterns between domestic and foreign visitors in a destination if they are both only visiting for the day or a few hours.

However, foreign visitors may be more likely to collect souvenirs which reflect local culture and the area than domestic tourists who may share the same core cultural background, values and identity. Although tourist origin may also be relevant in terms of actual spending power, not all domestic or foreign visitors display the same disposition towards holiday spending:

♦ some groups of visitors will come from areas (nationally or internationally) where the economy is stronger or perhaps weaker, and this will also influence their spending patterns;

- different types of international visitors are also likely to have different attitudes to the types of artefacts, souvenirs and services they will spend their money on.

The distinction is less significant for domestic tourism, albeit still relevant, but becomes more so when discussing the spending patterns of international tourists.

> ### *Where tourists come from can influence the type and intensity of impact*

In terms of social impact, point of origin is particularly relevant because it is the difference in socio-cultural background which is a key determinant in socio-cultural impacts. This often very much relates to how tourism is perceived in the destination and is reflected in the degree of contact with visitors and the age differences between the two groups:

- younger people tend to be more curious, adventurous and are more open to and accepting of change;

- younger people are more likely to make contact with visitors, perhaps by working in tourism-related facilities, and experience the features which distinguish the two differing cultures.

Point of origin is also relevant to environmental impacts, as different cultures can have differing attitudes and responses to both the natural and built environment:

- some plants and animals may be very special or significant to one culture, but merely peripheral to another;

- some cultures may place a much higher value on specific aspects of the natural or built environment which another culture may take for granted, or feel it is of little consequence.

In either case, how the visitor responds may have a significant impact on the resident population.

Length of Stay: Accommodation and food are two key elements of the long-stay spending pattern. Generally, the longer the visit, the greater the opportunity to spend and hence the higher level of economic impact:

♦ day-visitors tend to be the lower-spending tourist, due to how long they are actually in the destination, which affects their opportunity to shop.

> ***The length of stay can enhance as well as reduce the overall impact of tourism***

Day-visitors are also more likely to try to see as much as possible in terms of the environment and tourist facilities, rather than souvenir hunting or other forms of luxury shopping. Somewhere in the middle of the day-visit and long-stay market is the short-break visitor. This group may actually be the more beneficial, because the accommodation and catering outlets are used as they are with long-stay visitors:

♦ they have more time to explore, visit attractions and shop than the day-visitor, but they are also less likely to be concerned about stretching their money over the longer stay because they are only in the destination for a few days. Hence they spend more per person per day than the long-stay or day-visit tourist.

The importance of this market is witnessed in the significant growth in promoting city-break and short-break opportunities during the 1990s, which continue to expand.

Length of stay is also relevant to social and environmental impacts. Socially, tourists who stay longer will obviously have more time to meet the resident population, get to know them better and begin a process of cultural communication and understanding. In contrast short-stay visitors may make little or limited contact and not really get to know anything of where they are, which can also lead to misunderstanding, ignorance and even social intolerance from either group's point of view. Hence longer-stay visitors may have a significant impact by getting closer to the resident population, leaving a deeper and more lasting impression than the fleeting, superficial contact of the short-stay visitor.

Environmentally, length of stay may also influence the level of concern over ecological and environmental quality in the destination. Longer-stay visitors may develop an affinity with the place, showing greater concern for the impact they have on the structure and environment of the destination.

> *The reason for visiting a destination can affect the type and level of impact*

Purpose of Visit: Why people visit an area is also important to different types of tourism. Business travellers, on expense accounts, are likely to spend more per night than any other type of tourist. They will generally eat well, use extra services due to limited time and may indeed come back again in the future for a more leisurely holiday when time permits. However, if business tourists stay in accommodation and eat in restaurants which in themselves make little direct contribution to the destination economy (see points above), then there may be little difference in the level of impact. Similarly, people visiting and staying with friends or relatives in a destination (VFR tourists) tend to make a smaller contribution to the local economy, than tourists staying in commercial accommodation, because the costs of doing so have effectively been removed from the spending equation. They are less likely to eat out frequently in restaurants than if they were staying in a local hotel. Of course more food may have to be purchased by the host family which does contribute to the local economy in other ways.

Tourism and tourists come in many forms, shapes and sizes. Whether as holiday-makers, on business or just visiting friends and relatives, every community has tourists, and is affected by the industry in one way or another. Indeed, very few individuals (in the developed economies at least) are not directly or indirectly involved in tourism themselves, or contribute to its effect, either in receiving visitors in their community or as visitors themselves somewhere else. Whatever the reason for travel, wherever they come from, or how long they stay, all visitors contribute to the costs and benefits of tourism in a destination.

MAXIMIZING BENEFITS – MINIMIZING COSTS
Economic, social and environmental impacts are an inevitable element of tourism development. However, the extent to which they represent either a cost or a benefit will differ from place to place, and is dependent on many factors inside and outside the control of destination areas. This being said, there are several measures that can be taken which can help destinations influence the direction of tourism-induced change in a positive direction.

Economic Measures
The economic benefits of tourism in a destination area are primarily derived from the level of initial visitor spending which remains in the destination

economy after the cost of imports and other leakages have been removed. Thus one way of increasing the benefit is to *minimize the leaks*:

✓ Wherever possible, use local suppliers and wholesalers to provide goods and services used in tourism businesses – if they are initially uncompetitive, tell them and offer the opportunity to negotiate a better price;

✓ Encourage local suppliers and wholesalers to use other local producers and manufacturers to increase the destination supply chain further and help decrease leakages;

✓ Use local or locally based businesses' services when necessary (such as accountants, lawyers, planners, marketing and business consultants) – if they are initially uncompetitive, give them the opportunity to renegotiate;

✓ Use local or locally based financial services, such as building societies and credit unions, and seek to negotiate more favourable services and rates for local tourism businesses;

✓ Seek to provide incentives for local entrepreneurs and other interested parties to become more active participants in the tourism business;

✓ Seek to increase opportunities for shopping, particularly for arts, crafts and other luxury goods which are unique to the area, produced by local artisans or sourced by local suppliers;

✓ Encourage visitors to stay longer by increasing the diversity and range of activities and facilities (both ticketed and free) – this could also encourage the potential of future repeat visits as well;

✓ Take deliberate steps to encourage more specific (and higher-spending) tourist markets which are most appropriate to the destination (see Chapter 5);

✓ Take steps to upgrade current tourist products, offering greater value for money and encouraging a positive tourist experience;

✓ Encourage all tourism-related businesses to hire local people, not only as sales assistants and ticket agents, but as management staff as well;

✓ Use local construction firms, contractors, methods and materials wherever possible to reflect local character in the development of facilities and other attractions;

✓ Measure and monitor performance (see Chapter 9) to know what is working, what is not and where improvements can be made.

Socio-cultural Measures

Tourism can be a catalyst for change in a destination, but the extent, nature and direction of this change is not always predictable. There is no single or absolute socio-cultural change which results from tourism, and different people will respond and be affected in different ways. Socio-cultural impacts take time to develop and it is often difficult to define or distinguish change caused primarily by tourism, and that which may be the result of other sources of change. However, when the following methods are included in the overall development process, the costs and benefits should be more readily identified, acknowledged and managed:

✓ Plan and develop tourism based on the goals and priorities of the local destination (see Chapter 6);

✓ Encourage and develop tourism, and attract tourists which are most appropriate to the destination's resources and its people;

✓ Involve both the public and private sector in the development of tourism, to help maintain direction and quality in the products and services which reflect community interest and values;

✓ Inform the destination community of why visitors come to the area and encourage them to participate in local visitor activities;

✓ Provide opportunities for community participation in festivals and events, as this can enhance community pride and public interest;

✓ Provide the opportunity for local residents to use visitor facilities and attractions at a privileged rate during the off-season, as this not only allows them to experience and appreciate what visitors come to see, but gives something back to the community;

✓ Deal with the industry's current problems before seeking to develop tourism further – ignoring issues and complaints may only lead to more serious problems in the future;

✓ Encourage more responsible and appropriate tourist behaviour by informing visitors and tour operators of local customs and values with respect to culture and the environment;

✓ Develop a tourism public awareness programme to highlight both the costs and benefits of tourism to the destination, and the role the community plays in managing tourism's impacts;

✓ Develop some form of public recognition or award system for tourism businesses, employees and members of the public which highlights achievements, service excellence and reflects community spirit.

Environmental Measures

Any form of physical development activity, wherever and for whatever reason, creates a change in the environment in which it is set. The management of this change is essentially a question of trade-offs: one outcome may be seen as acceptable, while another may be totally incompatible with the development objective. Whether in areas of high scenic value, cultural interest, architectural significance or ecological importance, all destinations have a physical ability to absorb tourism activity beyond which the associated change will tend to be negative. In tourism, the trade-offs are most often associated with the number of visitors using an environment spatially and temporally. As a result, managing the environmental impacts of tourism is often one of controlling visitor numbers and behaviour, one way or another.

✓ Control the number and locations of access points, through the siting of car-parks, accommodation, and means of transport to and within a destination area;

✓ Restrict access through the use of tickets and reservations – limiting numbers to certain times of the day, month or year, the length of stay, or under other specific conditions of use;

✓ Use the price mechanism to influence time of use by increasing or decreasing the cost of visiting a destination through entrance fees, local tourist taxes, discounts and other incentives – this can both encourage or discourage different tourist markets;

✓ Use (or absence) of signposting to influence visitor behaviour, either to follow certain routes, highlight restrictions, inform and educate, or discourage casual visitors;

✓ Environmental hardening through the renovation and replacement of different aspects of the environment with more durable and/or less use-sensitive materials, such as boardwalks, paving and wood chip trails;

✓ 'Demarket' certain areas by producing promotional material which highlights other attractions and activities to influence usage patterns – offer alternative activities and sites which are more resilient to continued use;

✓ Use land-use zones spatially to identify areas for further development or certain types of activity, and others where any development or tourist use will be strictly limited or excluded – zoning can also be used to manage areas in time where different activities can use a space during different hours, days or seasons;

contd

✓ Develop new facilities, attractions and offer alternative
   activities away from areas already under pressure to help
   spread out the overall impact to the wider area and reduce
   potential problems in any one location (i.e. dispersion);
✓ Cluster attractions, amenities and visitor services in areas more
   able to cope with increased activity, possibly near destination
   entry points to discourage dispersal and draw off pressure from
   more fragile areas of the destination (i.e. 'honey-potting');
✓ Encourage the development of more environmentally sensitive
   and responsible forms of tourism and visitor activities – support
   tourism growth that is incremental, reflecting the priorities and
   objectives of the destination, which seeks to complement not
   compete with the destination's environmental setting.

WHERE TO NEXT?

Tourism can be a highly profitable industry, particularly at the national and
international level. The effect in local or regional destinations, however, can
be quite different with impacts highly dependent on local conditions and
proactive management. It is important to remember that tourism carries
with it both costs and benefits, and understanding these impacts is the first
step in developing a more successful and sustainable destination industry:

♦ tourism does create jobs, but it is no economic panacea – it is
   better suited to play a supporting rather then key role in a
   destination's economy;

♦ the more successful destinations are those where tourism is highly
   integrated in the local economy – goods and services supplied by
   local firms, attractions and facilities locally owned, and local
   residents employed at all levels;

♦ tourism development has an opportunity cost – it requires the use
   of resources and a commitment to long-term management that
   might be better directed elsewhere;

♦ environmental quality is a fundamental element of tourism and its
   planning must pay close attention to the setting to ensure the
   integrity of the resource is maintained;

♦ a receptive host community is an important feature of successful tourism development – resident annoyance or antagonism can lead to more serious social problems;

♦ many problems and issues can be resolved or reduced through comprehensive planning which takes account of various concerns – development can then be based on rational decision-making in the best interests of the destination.

Better planning and management of tourism is the key to an effective response to the issues discussed in this chapter. However, there is no universal solution which is equally effective in all situations. Each destination must decide for itself what is the most appropriate path for tourism development in their area. Getting organized, deciding what it is they want to develop, understanding their resources and their limitations, knowledge of their current and potential tourist markets, dealing with management issues and monitoring tourism's impacts are all fundamental to this end. This chapter has explained how differences in tourism supply and demand influence tourism impacts. Now the subsequent chapters will show how destinations can evaluate their own situation and seek to develop a positive tourism response.

FURTHER READING on Tourism Impacts

Economist Intelligence Unit (1992) *The Tourism Industry and the Environment*, Special Report No. 2453. London: Business International Limited.

Glasson, J., Godfrey, K. and Goodey, B. (1995) *Towards Visitor Impact Management*. Aldershot, UK: Avebury.

Hughes, H.L. (1994) 'Tourism multiplier studies: a more judicious approach', in *Tourism Management*, Vol. 15, No. 6, pp 403–406.

Mathieson, A. and Wall, G. (1982) *Tourism: economic, physical and social impacts*. London: Longman Group UK Limited.

Nelson, J. G., Butler, R. and Wall, G. (eds) (1993) *Tourism and Sustainable Development: monitoring, planning, managing*. Department of Geography Publications Series No. 37, University of Waterloo, Canada.

Ryan, C. (1991) *Recreational Tourism: a social science perspective*. London: Routledge.

Theobold, W. (ed) (1994) *Global Tourism: the next decade*. Oxford: Butterworth-Heinemann.

CHAPTER THREE

Where to start?
Fundamentals of tourism organization

INTRODUCTION

Successful tourism development will not simply happen on its own. It must be made to happen. To do so requires time and effort from both public and private sector interests to ensure development activity has a focus, based on policy, goals and objectives, not just some haphazard collection of disconnected ideas. Co-ordination is the key, and the key to co-ordination is getting organized, which generally means forming some sort of tourism association or committee to help lead tourism development activity in a particular direction. The destination's tourism association then becomes responsible for creating a positive tourism policy and beginning to prepare the destination's comprehensive tourism planning and management strategy.

Many destinations, however, probably have some form of tourism group already, and there are numerous examples of local groups actively supporting tourism in their area. Indeed, different political structures, history, tradition and statutory responsibility means there can be no single organizational structure suitable for all locations. Whatever form they take, however, one thing many groups have in common has been a tendency to focus efforts on advertising, promotions or the provision of information, rather than a more comprehensive approach to industry development and management. In addition, seldom have resident interests been actively involved in the tourism development discussion for their community.

Given the diversity of tourism destinations, it is not really valid to promote one form of organization over another. Yet whatever form they take, there are a number of core operations and activities which should be considered by all tourism groups, including *co-ordination and leadership, policy, marketing and communications, hospitality training and customer care* and *monitoring and research*. Each of these elements has an important role to play in the successful development and ongoing operation of tourism in a local destination. With this in mind, this chapter looks at the overall role and function of the tourism association in the planning and development of a successful and sustainable tourist destination.

THE TOURISM ORGANIZATION

There is no perfect prototype of a 'tourism association' to suit each and every destination. Indeed, the range of names used to describe tourism groups (e.g. *tourism board, association, committee, advisory group* or *visitor and convention bureau*), serves well to highlight the broad diversity of approach applied to the industry in many different locations. The name of course is not really that important, but rather it is the ability of the organization to manage and direct tourism development in the destination given the range and diversity of individuals, groups and businesses so often involved.

Traditionally, the role of tourism development has deferred to either a local Chamber of Commerce, or some form of economic development committee or agency within local government. Local government clearly has a role to play as they are ultimately accountable to the resident community for the use of public goods which so often form a core element of a destination's tourism product. Equally, though, the private sector must be involved as some aspects of tourism development are clearly more appropriate to commercial interests. However, neither approach in isolation has really ever taken a comprehensive view of tourism, partly due to their own specific interests, but also because of the multifaceted and fragmented nature of tourism, which makes the co-ordination of development activity sometimes a little difficult.

Yet tourism does not function as a separate or distinct sector of the economy, and it should not be planned as such. Tourism development needs to be the work of all community interests if it is to make a significant contribution to the destination without all the negative baggage it potentially includes. This means involving all sectors of the destination in the planning and management function, drawing representation from:

♦ local resident groups;

♦ regional or national government;

♦ regional tourism groups;

♦ special interest community groups;

- business groups (e.g. Chamber of Commerce); as well as,

- local government;

- commercial interests;

- external consultant advisers (where necessary).

A role exists for all of these in a tourism group at one level or another. Without them the group will not necessarily have the collective skills, knowledge or expertise to ensure all interests are considered in the preparation and application of a comprehensive tourism development strategy.

Setting up a tourism association could involve the expansion of an existing local group, the creation of an entirely new group, or some combination of the current structure within a new framework. Ideally, this grouping of tourism interests should be lead by a core team of nine to twelve members, drawing representation from a cross-section of the destination's broad tourism interests. Members should be selected (or invited) to participate in this core team on the basis of their:

- knowledge and experience of the destination area;

- commitment to the fostering of tourism opportunities;

- ability to remain objective and take a comprehensive view of the work;

- ability to invest enough time and energy to get things done;

- ability to work constructively with other people.

A model for a destination tourism group is presented in Figure 3.1. The objective of the model is not to suggest some rigid organizational structure, but rather graphically to illustrate the important connections between private, public (government) and community interests in the planning and management of tourism. The principle being to foster the integration of tourism concerns with other socio-economic issues, and assure that tourism is considered more effectively in land-use planning as a development issue, and not simply as promotional activity. The tourism association acts as a catalyst and facilitator for the diversity of local interests, by channelling information, research and ideas to and from local government committees, private sector interests and the resident community. Whatever format it takes, however, the tourism group should be a formal organization through which the destination's tourism programme is built.

Notwithstanding its membership, size or origin, the success of any tourism group will very much depend on the individual and collective competence and commitment of those directly involved actually to plan and manage the industry. It will also depend on the legitimacy of the group in representing all destination interests in the function of managing tourism development. With this in mind, the tourism group should not be seen as simply another sub-committee of local government, or the local Chamber of Commerce. While it may obviously have close links with both government and commerce, it should also have its own sense of identity and purpose, based on strong leadership and co-ordination of the destination's tourism industry.

Figure 3.1: Model Participants in a Local Destination Tourism Group

Co-ordination and Leadership

Tourism is a highly diverse and fragmented industry, with possible connections to most sectors of the economy. Co-ordinating these different interests and leading them in a unified direction is a core task of any tourism group. The question of leadership discussed here, however, is not necessarily about individual character or personality, but rather the collective ability of the organization to offer some form of focus and direction to the development strategy process. While individual effort is obviously important, a key element in preparing any tourism strategy is having the right group in place to develop and implement the plan.

The initial drive for tourism development will often emerge from individual entrepreneurs or a special interest group, however, tourism leadership should not be consolidated in one person *per se*, but should be a shared responsibility. Group interaction which is positive and forward-looking can provide an effective steer to the exercise of leadership. This does not mean that groups and individuals will never disagree, but rather collective decision-making, based on a broad base of opinion and support will more likely arrive at an acceptable solution than if developed from only one perspective. The interaction amongst people in different professional roles, each with their own perspective, can provide the motivation and guidance for tourism development much better than a single sector approach.

In whatever form or structure the tourism group exists, there are a few points on leadership and co-ordination which need to be recognized and understood, as they can significantly influence the group's efforts. These include *potential objection* from members of the destination community (residential, political or commercial), *current interests* of those already involved in tourism, and *resident involvement* in the tourism development process.

Potential Objection: Not everyone will always be happy with tourism development and will make their feelings known both in public and in private. Potential objection to a new tourism initiative can arise from any number of directions, and all tourism groups at some point in time will face some form of opposition. It may be an objection to the types of proposed activity, the style of development, or any number of different reasons. In some cases, the level and intensity of objection can lead to project abandonment, or require a significant rethink of core objectives. In others it may just need better explanation and articulation of the development goals. Whatever the case, in terms of leadership, the tourism group needs to be aware of potential objections, understand why they have arisen, or could potentially develop in different circumstances, and be prepared to compromise and where possible bring the objectors on board.

Current Interests: It is important that any new attempts to organize and co-ordinate tourism development activity should take account of what already exists to ensure these interests are incorporated in any new structure or association. It is possible that some form of tourism group may already exist in the destination but is not officially recognized or it exists as a loose collection of like-minded individuals but lacks any formal structure.

It may be that someone else is already trying better to co-ordinate current efforts and a totally new approach would be unwarranted. One of the key problems in creating a tourism group is the very real danger that it may alienate or adversely affect those already working on tourism initiatives. It is vital therefore in terms of co-ordination and leadership that all those already committed to the cause are identified and invited to continue their efforts as part of a new tourism team.

Resident Involvement: This represents a third core element of the successful co-ordination and leadership of tourism development activity. Resident and wider community support for tourism is an essential element of any development strategy. As tourism destinations tend to put the whole 'community' on show (selling its history, culture and environment) it has the very real potential to impact upon all who live and work in that destination. Community involvement in the strategy and management process is a central aspect of minimizing tourism impacts as they affect the resident population. Such involvement also provides the opportunity for constructive criticism of issues directly affecting destination residents; it can help to diffuse local tensions that might otherwise develop into major problems for tourism growth; and it can help achieve more broad-based political support when actions are shown to have considered local concerns and taken an appropriate response.

Effective co-ordination and leadership are vital components of any tourism development process. They help promote flexibility in terms of generating new ideas, solving current issues, helping to avoid the problem of general overlap of energy and ideas, and seek to avoid the unnecessary duplication of effort. They can also help to identify weaknesses in current operations, and direct efforts towards the realization of the destination's tourism policy.

Tourism Policy

Setting a tourism policy is a key stage in the tourism strategy process, and one of the vital first actions that any tourism group should undertake. The destination's tourism policy is meant to guide subsequent actions in a way with which the destination feels comfortable. It represents the managerial framework through which present and future tourism issues are analysed and decisions taken. In this sense, policy is a bit like the values held by individuals: some types of development activity we would be happy to see take place, whereas some others may prove unpopular and conflict with what we feel is right or proper in that setting.

No matter what the level of discussion (i.e. local, regional or national), policy is what determines development goals and objectives, providing general guidelines for tourism actions and activity. While actual policy issues may differ from place to place, it is policy which drives all other aspects of tourism supply and demand. Tourism policy effectively points the way by stating in general terms what the destination would like to see happen, what it is prepared to tolerate and what will not be acceptable.

The destination's tourism policy statement should be prepared and formally recognized by the tourism group and the local government for the area. This may be as part of a local planning statement, or land-use development plan or a special resolution of the local government, formally to recognize tourism and the actions of the tourism group. Policy statements can range from a simple declaration of intent, to very detailed and long drawn-out documents with several sections, clauses and subclauses. The latter tends to be true more of national and regional statements than the more localized destination policy. Generally, the larger the area or higher the level of administration, the more lengthy and wide-ranging the policy statements are, and the more self-important sounding they become as well.

To start with, policy statements should be positive, concise and to the point. While it is possible to have negative policies, within the field of tourism they are inclined to have a more positive bent, suggesting the encouragement of tourism rather than its cessation. For example:

> Tourism makes a positive contribution to ... (*the community*) ... through the creation of jobs for local residents, and the provision of additional facilities which adds to local quality of life. The continued development of tourism will therefore be encouraged where it is seen to lead to further improvements in the quality of the visitor experience, the facilities available for their use, encourage them to stay longer and ensure any adverse social, economic and/or environmental impacts are minimized.

A more detailed policy statement might break these points down and be a little more specific. The policy statement may open with an indication of the general reasons for supporting tourism (e.g. its contribution to the economy, a wealth of natural attractions, its educational value, quality of life arguments and civic pride) and then move on to a series of specific points indicating how tourism issues will be viewed and addressed. For example:

- ♦ to encourage tourism according to the principles of sustainable development, ensuring a balanced approach in harmony with the destination's economic, social and environmental goals;

- ♦ to use tourism to stimulate the expansion and production of creative artwork from local artisans and craftspeople;

- ♦ to develop tourism which helps conserve the destination's unique sense of heritage by promoting the use and redevelopment of local historic buildings and sites;

- ♦ to encourage local entrepreneurs to initiate development ideas which may lead to new tourism attractions and new jobs for local people;

- ♦ to provide tourists with a quality and efficient information service;

- ♦ to promote a form of tourism which fosters greater understanding and respect for local customs, values and religious beliefs;

- ♦ to ensure the protection of natural areas and the conservation of local archaeological and cultural artefacts;

- ♦ to ensure the health and safety of visitors and their belongings;

- ♦ to ensure tourism issues and interest are considered by all local agencies in their discussions and to standardize basic support and policy on tourism;

- ♦ to monitor on a regular basis the impact of tourism on the local quality of life and the natural environment, and to take corrective actions where possible;

- ♦ to encourage the development of education and training programmes for tourism personnel in aspects of customer care and hospitality.

Tourism policy lays the basic philosophy for development and effectively sets a map for the future of tourism in the destination. However, it is far too easy to get bogged down in arguments over policy detail and never get anything else done. It is not really worth spending too much time debating the finer points of policy, because they are only as good as the goals, objectives and actions which stem from them. While it is clearly necessary to get the policy right, it is how that policy is used to generate and direct actual development activity which will really judge its worth. Indeed, policy statements should be dynamic and able to respond to changing circumstances in both supply and demand. They can then be adjusted or rewritten to take account of chang-ing needs, issues or as new opportunities arise. This does not mean, of course, that policy should be so flexible as to offer no long-term direction, but rather it should be continuously reviewed and revised (where necessary) as conditions and issues affecting tourism continue to change. After all, the best policy for today may not be the best policy for tomorrow.

Setting policy is only one aspect of the group's activities and other core operational areas include: *marketing and communications, hospitality train-ing and customer care,* and *monitoring and research.* Each of these three broad areas are well suited to be taken up by special sub-committees of the tourism organization. Sub-committees or working groups are used to devel-op and report on various tourism issues. They may be permanent and look at a particular topic on a regular basis, or *ad hoc,* set up only to look at specific issues as and when they arise and then disperse when that issue is resolved.

Although members of the organization's core team should lead and direct the sub-groups, individual interest and enthusiasm, the type and level of work, and their concurrent nature suggests they are best dealt with through a series of interrelated sub-committees. These working groups would then seek to gather further support and participation from local resident and busi-ness interests to generate ideas and solutions as well as enthusiasm.

Marketing and Communications

Far too often, tourism marketing is seen by many as simply promotions and advertising. While these topics clearly fall under the broad marketing agen-da, they represent only one aspect of the marketing and communications function of the tourism group. Demand for tourism is dynamic and if des-tinations are to stay in touch with the market they must continuously reassess their activities. The destination which does not take account of changing trends and responds in kind may find itself unable to maintain its market share or position. To be sustainable, tourism groups need actively to identify the type of tourist they would like to come to the destination. However, this means much more than simply looking around to see who is visiting the area now. It requires ongoing effort in developing a detailed understanding of the different types of tourist markets, their travel preferences, their likes and dislikes, where they come from and their travel needs in order to help identify which groups of tourists bring greatest benefit and minimal cost to the destination, both now and in the future (see Chapter 5). As one of its ongoing functions a marketing sub-group should seek to:

♦ identify groups of tourists they are able to satisfy better than competing destinations which help the destination to achieve its tourism goals;

♦ undertake research and creative thought on building profiles of different tourist segments that the destination could consider trying to attract;

♦ define the criteria used to decide which tourist segments are best suited to the destination;

♦ develop a portfolio of tourist groups which will be targeted in promotional activity, and review this over time and adjust as necessary.

Similarly, the tourism group that restricts its assessment to existing groups without exploring potential new opportunities runs the very real risk of market stagnation and even decline, all to the detriment of local tourism. A tourist destination will only remain competitive if tourism groups are proactive in their approach to marketing and the co-ordination of communication activities.

Communication is effectively the means and medium through which potential visitors are made aware of the destination and what it has to offer (e.g. advertising, public relations, sales promotions, personal selling and the printed word – see Chapter 7). It is very easy in a diverse industry such as tourism for a destination to have many different channels of communication. One danger of this is that not all forms or channels, however, will put across the same message, which can lead to confusion, disappointment and ultimately a poor image of the destination. Thus another function of the marketing sub-group is to ensure that the variety of techniques and sources of information used in communications are pulling in the same direction and putting across a similar general message about the destination. While the specific details for different attractions and services will vary accordingly, the core 'theme' they present should be the same. In addition to the points above, this relates to the co-ordination of pedestrian and vehicle signposting in and around the destination, the display and function of information and interpretation panels, the quality and distribution of tourist literature (maps, brochures and guidebooks) and the quality of information provided through customer service people in the destination. This latter point being a key function of the sub-group on hospitality training and customer care.

Hospitality Training and Customer Care

Tourism is a service industry and so much of the business is based on the quality of the tourist's experience in the destination. Therefore a second core function of the tourism group must be in the area of hospitality training particularly as this concerns issues of customer care (see Chapter 8). Tourism is a highly competitive industry where the quality of service and attention to detail play an ever-increasing role in successful tourism development. Unfortunately for some destinations all the effort is focused on providing hotels, restaurants and visitor attractions, but without taking a really good look at the quality of service any of these provide. In these settings the destination tries very hard to attract new visitors in, but fails to recognize the value of their current market and does nothing to encourage them back.

As tourism is in the business of hospitality, methods of training and informing those people who will most frequently come into contact with visitors are vitally important. Any tourism group needs seriously to consider how hospitality training will be incorporated in the ongoing tourism development process. By paying closer attention to the detail of customer care and the quality of the tourist experience, the destination will be in a much better position to:

♦ generate a higher level of repeat and referred business which are considered a vital component of any destination's long-term success;

♦ enhance tourist satisfaction, which can help to increase the length of stay and lead to positive recommendations from previously satisfied visitors;

♦ develop that unique sense of place, which makes the destination stand out as the best place to visit amongst its direct competitors over the longer term.

However, a major problem with customer care training is the reluctance of both employers and employees to see the merit of improving skills in communication and behaviour, or knowledge and understanding of the local tourist product. Some people fail to see how providing a better service could lead to better business for themselves. In particular they fail to see the link between the short-term cost of training and the long-term benefit of better customer service. Employees, too, are sometimes hesitant to participate, because, after all, they already know how to answer the phone and greet people – and deal with complaints? Unfortunately, while many aspects of customer care can boil down to basic courtesy and common sense, far too often these core personal skills are not honed to their full potential.

It is important for all employees who may come into contact with visitors (including management) to understand the issues of hospitality, and it is vital for front-line customer service staff to be well versed in the techniques and methods of customer care. After all, it is these people who sell the service to the tourist and receive the complaints when something goes wrong. The tourism organization therefore needs to take the lead in promoting the need for, and opportunity to improve the skills of people who will and are dealing with tourists on a day-to-day basis. They need to convince employers that this is good for the health of their business and the overall success of tourism in the destination. This point can be partially achieved through the collection of data showing the value of satisfied customers versus the costs which poor service can create, which is all a part of monitoring and research.

Monitoring and Research

The tourism development process is dynamic. It is not a one-shot attempt at putting together a master plan and then sitting back while it all happens. To do so would be indefensible in terms of deciding what has worked and what has not. Early on in the development process the tourism group needs to establish a system which will allow for the regular and ongoing evaluation of development decisions; what may have been valid at some point in the past may no longer be true today. Monitoring tells us what has happened, what is happening, and what could happen given different alternatives. This type of information is the basis of good decision-making, and research is the foundation of good information. Therefore, a third core function of the tourism group must be in the monitoring of development activity and tourist satisfaction (see Chapter 9). Monitoring and research should be carried out on all aspects of the development programme, including:

♦ measuring any changes in the effect tourism has had on the quality and integrity of local resources;

♦ reviewing development planning applications on the basis of their potential benefit to visitors and where possible to residents as well;

- assessing possible changes in the level of resident hospitality towards visitors;

- evaluating overall and specific levels of tourist satisfaction in the destination;

- measuring the economic impact of tourism on employment and income generation;

- evaluating the impact of specific marketing activities on increasing visitor numbers in different target markets.

The actual type and level of information to be collected will, of course, depend on the destination and the type of development activity taking place. However, monitoring should be done on a regular and formal basis, with brief factual reports written and submitted to the tourism group on each objective of the development strategy. These reports should contain information on:

- the key issue being addressed and the goal to which it relates;

- the specific objectives of the actions being taken;

- a description of the results and how far objectives have been met;

- a comment on what remedial action may be appropriate and actions taken (if necessary).

The purpose of this exercise is to present the tourism group with the opportunity regularly to assess its progress towards achieving its long-term goals, and make adjustments where current actions are not addressing core concerns.

SUMMARY

The key to the success of destination tourism development is the co-ordination and leadership provided by a good tourism organization. The actual size and sophistication of this group will vary from place to place, but whatever the structure, if the group takes effective charge of the tourism planning and management function, the destination should be in a better position to achieve a more sustainable tourism industry. Through an adaptive process of compromise this management structure should mean that tourism planning and management will become more:

♦ **Comprehensive** – with social, environmental, economic and political elements of the tourism system incorporated as part of a holistic approach to local industry management;

♦ **Iterative and dynamic** – with tourism issues considered on a regular basis, and where decisions are made on a full understanding of the present situation, and problems of the past fed back into future deliberations;

♦ **Systematic** – where the long-term and structured process of evaluation and review is fed into the planning process;

♦ **Integrative** – with tourism interests incorporated into other local government committees, and with industry components able to discuss areas of mutual benefit, so reducing needless expenditure;

♦ **Community-oriented** – with working groups drawing representation from public interest groups, resident groups and business associations;

♦ **Renewable** – with tourism activity considered a part of the local socio-economic system and does not prejudice the integrity of local resources;

♦ **Goal-oriented and implementable** – with community concerns considered alongside business enthusiasm, and with public administration channelling entrepreneurial spirit towards a policy and strategy acceptable to the community.

But of course, getting organized is really only the beginning of the tourism strategy process. Once the group is in place the destination is now ready to begin seriously to evaluate its resources and tourism potential (see Chapter 4), develop a more thorough understanding of its current and potential tourism markets (see Chapter 5), and then begin to prepare the actual development strategy and marketing plan (see Chapters 6 and 7).

FURTHER READING *for Getting Organized*

Edgell, D.L. (1990) *International Tourism Policy*. New York: Van Nostrand Reinhold.
Gunn, C.A. (1988) *Tourism Planning* (2nd edition). New York: Taylor & Francis.
Mill, R.C. and Morrison, A. M. (1985) *The Tourism System: an introductory text*.
    London: Prentice-Hall International.

CHAPTER FOUR

What have we got?
Understanding tourism resources

INTRODUCTION

A destination's tourism resource base is the essence of that location's tourism appeal. Tourism resources are all, and any, of those features which draw people in to a destination. They form the core of visitor attractions, but also include other services and facilities which cater to accommodate and entertain tourists while in the destination area. Tourism resources represent the supply side of the basic supply-and-demand equation, which needs to be to matched with market demand to develop a successful tourism destination. They are the 'pulling power', that serve to attract specific groups of tourists (see Chapter 5).

A thorough understanding of both supply and demand is a vital element of any tourism development process. Far too often, however, when areas begin to plan for tourism development a first course of action is directed simply at trying to bring people in. This tends to follow a scant review of what a place can offer, but without a clear understanding of how these resources fit together or what the destination could realistically hope to achieve. The task of assessing the area's real tourism potential (i.e. resource quality, accessibility and pull) is often overlooked in favour of the more immediate and glamorous activity of advertising and promotion.

Even in current destinations, evaluating tourism supply is an important step in the development process. It helps destinations to identify product gaps, expose weak links in services and establish development priorities. It is also very useful later on when it comes to the production of tourist directories, information services and future promotion or communications programmes. Unfortunately, some destinations feel they already know what they have and believe growth will be achieved simply through more forceful selling.

However, a proper development strategy in any setting requires up-to-date and accurate information on tourism supply, and without this no amount of promotion will ever make up for a lack of basic tourism resources. Thus a fundamental step for any area seeking to develop or improve its tourism appeal, is critically to evaluate their tourism resource base. In the pursuit of this task this chapter explains the main steps of the *tourism resource audit* as a critical review of a destination's tourism supply.

TYPES OF TOURISM RESOURCES

Tourism resources come in all shapes and sizes, and most features of an area can be considered part of the overall tourism resource base of a destination. They include elements of the natural and man-made environment, festivals and events, activities, purpose-built facilities, hospitality and transport services. These features are classified as either *principal* or *supporting resources*.

Principal Resources are those which have the strongest pulling power, and usually represent the key motivating factor in the tourist's travel decision process.

Supporting Resources are those which supplement a destination's principal resources and contribute to the destination's visitor appeal, but do not on their own represent a prime motive for travel.

Categorizing resources under any heading, however, inevitably requires some degree of discretion. Often there will be some overlap between the type of categories and the relative importance of these resources to different visitor markets. What may be a *cultural* resource to one may be considered a *festival* or *special event* to another. Indeed, how someone categorizes a resource can very much depend on how they view the destination and the type of tourism activity on offer (for example, Concorde is just a *transport service* to some, but it may be considered a *core attraction* to another). Similarly, what is a *principal resource* for some, may be considered by others as supplementary or play only a *supporting role* in the destination's tourism appeal. Resources can also have a wide, universal appeal (e.g. a natural vista) or be more specialist and appeal to only a specific market (e.g. the birthplace of some famous or obscure person).

In fact not all destinations actually have a principal resource *per se*, but rather an amalgam of supporting resources which when combined form a 'synthetic' principal attraction. On their own, environmental setting (natural or not), local culture or the services available may not be enough to draw visitors in, but when combined they form an attraction base or image which becomes the principal resource. In many towns and smaller cities it is often this amalgam of resources which creates the tourism appeal or image which serves to attract people to that particular place.

Given the likely overlap and wide mix of resources that make up the travel industry, the number of potential categories and subcategories to describe them is virtually endless. However, for the sake of simplicity, this book uses five categories to describe the tourism resource base: *natural*, *cultural*, *events*, *activities* and *services*. Each of these groups has a number of subheadings which help further to classify different aspects of these broad lead categories. The following sections are meant to be exemplary, although not exhaustive, of the types of features which could be considered under each of these five categories. The tables are not absolute and each destination will need to adjust or add to them as appropriate to their own tourism setting. However, they do encompass a wide range of resource possibilities which commonly feature in tourism destinations.

Natural Resources

These include aspects of land and landscape such as mountains or other geographical phenomena, wildlife species, birds or rare plants and water features such as a lakes, rivers or waterfalls. They often form a central element of a destination's tourism appeal. In some locations this may even be the most important destination feature (e.g. coastal resorts, ski hills). Climate also plays a key role, both as an overriding factor in terms of seasonal change and influence on other natural resources, but also with its influence on other resource categories (i.e. when certain festivals take place, ski season, etc.).

Natural resources are an invaluable tourism asset and are fundamental to the development of tourism for virtually all destinations. They tend to be the foundation from which other resources are developed, and thus often play both a principal and key supporting role in tourism development. However, natural resources also tend to be the least productive on their own in terms of direct economic benefit especially when in 'public' ownership (see Chapter 2). In addition, they are frequently considered a free resource as ownership can be difficult to define, making them more difficult to manage in terms of visitor impacts unless their use can be specifically regulated. Figure 4.1 lists a number of common natural resource elements frequently included in various destination lists of attractions.

NATURAL

FLORA

forested areas; orchards – hard & soft fruit; specialist farms; trees – autumn foliage, first growth conifers; vineyards; wilderness; wild flowers – meadows; rare/endangered; spices & herbs.

LANDSCAPE

beaches; causeways; caves; cliffs; coral reef; desert; unique land forms; geological formations – glacial, wind, rain; gorge/canyon; islands; mountains; plains; spits; sand dunes; semiprecious gemstones; swampland; valleys & plateaux; volcanoes.

FAUNA

birds – aquatic, large/birds of prey, rare/endangered; insects; wildlife – large/big game, small, rare/ endangered, marine mammals; domesticated.

CLIMATE

seasonal – spring (blossoms), summer (dry/humid), autumn (foliage), winter (snow); arid; temperate; tropical; continental; coastal; alpine; wind.

WATER

rivers – slow meander, rapids, cataracts; lakes; estuaries; thermal springs; geysers; springs/wells; waterfalls; ocean/sea; snow/ice.

Figure 4.1: Index of Natural Resource Elements

Cultural Resources

These cover a wide variety of features including aspects of both past and present lifestyles, attitudes and social settings. They include elements of history *in situ*, such as old buildings and ruins, castles, forts and historic homes. They include elements of historical interpretation based on fact and artefact, such as museums, heritage sites and other interpretative centres. They also include the man-made or urban fabric of many historic towns and cities. In fact an attractive built environment is an important feature of most destinations. Even in natural settings, the quality of built facilities is a signif- icant feature.

Cultural resources reflect certain aspects of current society and how people from different areas and ethnic origin live, work and play. They include religious settings, elements of nationality and other aspects of the life and lifestyle of a particular indigenous culture and society. They also include such things as the site of significant events, or the location of some popular social phenomena, for example, a famous film setting, or where a television series was shot. Most of the aspects in this category, as with those of natural resources, have become a tourism resource out of consequence rather than as a result of their original function or primary intent (see Figure 4.2).

CULTURAL

RELIGIOUS

mosques; synagogues; temples; churches – cathedrals, chapels, missionaries, frontier/pioneer; burial grounds; shrines; pilgrimage sites; other religions.

HERITAGE

castles; forts; historic birthplace; historic building; historic home; historic settings – cottages, mansions, villages/towns, ghost towns, folklore; museums – modern, antiquities, specialist collections, anomalies, science/technical; monuments; ancient/derelict ruins – aboriginal, indigenous, prehistoric, Bronze Age, Celtic, Roman, Norman, Renaissance, Medieval, Industrial Revolution; interpretation centres; landmarks; battle sites; ancient roads or paths.

OTHER

ethnic celebrations; indigenous culture – dance, dress, language/dialect, food & drink, music, art, work & industry, craft work; archaeological sites; TV series location; famous residents; folklore; local traditions.

Figure 4.2: Index of Cultural Resource Elements

Event Resources

The events category presents a vast array of festivals, tournaments and business activities which serve both a tourist and separate business function. Many regular events have their origins in some social or cultural activity initially designed to serve a resident market, but which has grown to become either a principal or supporting tourism resource attraction. These may include street carnivals, parades or other ethnic celebrations. They may also include competitions in sport, recreation, music or the arts. These events, if they happen on a regular basis, can help form an image of the destination, creating the synthetic principal resource out of many smaller supporting features. However, events are only really useful as a tourism resource if they are of a sufficient scale actually to draw visitors in, or be of enough interest to supplement visitor activities while in the destination.

EVENTS

FESTIVALS

music – jazz, folk, country, brass, classical, popular, local; drama/theatre; dance – classical ballet, contemporary, national, folk; wine/food; literature/poetry.

TOURNAMENTS

sports – local, regional, national, international; athletics; racing – horses, dogs, cars/motor bikes.

BUSINESS

trade shows – agricultural, boat, automobile, recreational vehicle, sports equipment; conventions – business, clubs/organizations.

OTHER

re-enactments; nationality days; ethnic celebrations; street carnivals; rodeos; parades; art and craft fairs; agricultural fair; flower shows; auctions; antique fairs; religious pilgrimage; pet shows/contests; fishing contest; regattas; air show/tattoos; military displays; photo exhibitions; celebrity visits.

Figure 4.3: Index of Event Resource Elements

Events also encompass larger, high-profile but less frequent activities, such as major trade shows, business conventions and national and international sporting events. These types of events serve to highlight a destination for short periods of time, drawing in large visitor numbers but for a limited duration. They often help to promote an area, particularly during the build up to the event, but once it is over the image can tend to fade and may not really affect future levels of tourist visitation. Figure 4.3 lists a number of general event categories which could be broken down into a virtually endless list of local variations on a theme.

Activity Resources

The 'activity' category on the whole tends to include what many traditionally define as the more purpose-built tourist/leisure attractions and facilities. These include theme parks and entertainment centres, zoos, aquariums, gardens and some other 'park'-type settings. Activity resources also encompass all those features of a destination which provide the visitor with the opportunity to participate in some form of recreational activity such as sport, leisure shopping, or even business and industry.

In terms of sport and recreation, activity resources range from ski hills, golf-courses or sports stadiums, to the less developed aspects such as nature trails, cycle routes or natural panoramic view points. As far as business or industry are concerned, these resources may include conference centres and meeting rooms, factory tours, and retail opportunities of some primary resource providers (e.g. farm shops, 'fisherman's wharf', etc.). In addition other commercial retail functions such as art and craft galleries, gift shops and other 'luxury' goods offer various opportunities for leisure shopping which is a key element of any destination's resource base.

Activity resources often represent both principal and supporting elements. For the potential long-stay visitor, the range and diversity of activities available can be a major motivating factor in choosing the destination. For others, however, it may simply be the quality of one particular activity which represents the major tourist 'pull', such as hiking trails or the ski hill. For the day and short-stay market, the overall diversity may still be important, but it may be the opportunity for leisure shopping which will sometimes characterize a destination's principal resource attraction, affecting destination choice. Figure 4.4 lists a number of facilities, services and recreational opportunities included as activities.

ACTIVITIES

RECREATIONAL

children's playground; golf-course – championship, driving range, 9/18 hole; ski hill/dry slope; tennis-courts; nature trails; hiking trails; horse trails; bike trails; bowling greens; canals; roller-blading; national games; flying/gliding; hang-gliding; parachuting; ballooning; horse riding; hobby/skills – painting, writing; view points; sports stadium; playing fields; ice rink; swimming-pool; water sports – canoeing, boating, river/canal boats, sailing, windsurfing, surfing, diving/snorkelling, whitewater rafting; fishing; hunting & shooting; caving/potholing; archery; off-road driving; fad & fashion activities; bungee jumping; white-knuckle activity.

SERVICES

retail – outfitters, camping supplies, winter sports, water sports; art galleries; craft galleries; speciality clothes; porcelain/china; glass; factory seconds/rejects; theatres; cinemas; health resorts; conference centre; meeting rooms.

FACILITIES

winery – tours/tasting, sales; zoo/sealife centre; wildlife sanctuary; game park; farm park; aviary; aquarium; arboretum; botanical garden; planetarium; theme park – amusement, water; mini/crazy golf; industrial tours – dams, hydro power, nuclear, mines, manufacturing; dockyards – naval, historic; wharves/piers – 'fisherman's wharf'; railways – funicular, steam; parks – local/public, regional, national.

Figure 4.4: Index of Activity Resource Elements

Service Resources

The final, but by no means least important set of tourism resources includes all those services in a destination which effectively makes tourism possible. These include the more obvious features of accommodation and catering, but also aspects of transport, hospitality and general community services. As a service resource transport features go beyond basic taxi and bus services to embrace opportunities ranging from bicycle and scooter rental to local airports and basic flying services. They also consider the provision of infrastructure which affects accessibility to the destination and personal mobility once the tourist has arrived.

Reception is another significant service resource for tourism. It is a collection of service functions which make travel easier, more efficient and hopefully engender a positive tourist experience. They are not usually principal resources, but still play a fundamental supporting role in the overall tourism supply. These include visitor information services (maps, brochures and interpretation), language and currency services, and community attitudes towards visitor activity. Visitor reception is thus another key element of a destination's image, which is fundamental to development because most tourists will not want to visit a place with a negative image, or which has a reputation for being 'less than friendly' towards outsiders (see Chapter 2).

Finally, general community services make up the rest of this category.

These would include, for example, health, public safety and security, emergency repair and general domestic supplies which may be used by tourists (see Figure 4.5).

Clearly not all of these resources are available in all locations. If they were, there would seem little point in travel, given the premiss of tourism as being the desire to see and experience someplace different. Each destination needs to examine its own resources and decide if, where, when and how these could be used in the tourism development process. However, one of the more difficult aspects in the planning of tourism is for communities and regions to recognize their total resource potential and the attendant opportunities and constraints this may place on tourism development in the area. Some resources may not be easy to identify at first, because many local features may seem basic and taken for granted by the destination. Yet what may seem of little consequence can actually be a key 'pulling' force or support mechanism in the destination's overall appeal. With this in mind, the *tourism resource audit* is designed to help destinations answer this development question: *What is it about this place that will make tourists want to come here?*

SERVICES*

TRANSPORT
access – road, rail, sea/river/canal, air; taxi – road, water; rental – car, aircraft, bicycle, horse (& carriage), scooter/moped, snowmobile, boat (canoe/kayak, row boat, sail boat, speed boat); rickshaw service; local tour bus; local airport – flying lessons, gliding; stables/equestrian.

ACCOMMODATION
hotels – 2–3 star, 4–5 star; B+B/guest-houses; self-catering units; caravans/trailers – static, touring; campgrounds; educational/dormitories; guest ranch; farm cottages; time share; inns & pubs; motels; youth hostels.

RECEPTION
information centre – maps, brochures, souvenirs; interpretation; town trails; language services; pedestrian signposting; display board maps; tours – local guides, self-directed; image/town theme; community attitudes; government policy; tour operators.

CATERING
bars/pubs; bistros/wine bars; coffee shop/tea room; fast food; takeaway/takeout; fine dining; family restaurants; ethnic cuisine; international cuisine; picnic sites; street vendors; self-service.

SERVICES
boat yard – overnight mooring, boat chandlers, repairs; car repair; petrol stations; banks – cash machines, currency exchange; police/security; medical services – doctor, ambulance, accident/emergency, first aid; veterinary services; general hardware; domestic supplies; communications – postal, telephone; energy supply; water supply; sewerage services.

Figure 4.5: Index of Service Resource Elements
*Services are sometimes referred to as 'tourism infrastructure'.

TOURISM RESOURCE AUDIT

The tourism resource audit is a structured and systematic two-stage process of *inventory* and *evaluation*:

Stage 1
involves a detailed listing of all resources which have some connection with tourism;

Stage 2
involves a critical evaluation of those resources in terms of their quality, uniqueness and tourist appeal, and a preliminary identification of those which need improving.

The overall objective of the audit is to create a comprehensive database of resources which will then be used to establish a tourism development strategy, including immediate and long-term development priorities, product improvements and future promotional activity (see Chapters 6 and 7). The resource audit, however, is not just the simple listing of resources, but a detailed analysis of a destination's tourism strengths and weaknesses from a supply perspective. Preparing the audit will require the time and effort of a number of people to ensure the database covers the entire spectrum of tourism opportunities and constraints in the area. Although the production of an audit may seem a little tedious, it is essential to establish a baseline from which the success of development activity can be measured. The effort put in at this stage should be well rewarded later on with the development of a more successful and sustainable tourism destination.

STAGE 1 – Resource Inventory

The first step in developing a resource inventory is essentially that of a brainstorming exercise. Key questions to consider when thinking about an area's tourism potential include:

♦ what could a visitor see in this area which might be of interest?

♦ what are the different types of attractions they could visit?

♦ what types of services would they require?

♦ what different activities could they do during their stay?

♦ if staying overnight, what accommodation is available?

Tourism resources should be listed by type as described above, and include all those features of the destination which currently are, or could be used by visitors. These lists should also include features outside the immediate local area, as regional resources will help draw people into a destination as well. However, to keep this 'region' within a destination context, the surrounding area to be included should be limited to a 20- to 30-minute drive time away from the core community. Clearly there will be some overlap between categories. For example, a steam railway is obviously a form of transport, but it is more likely to represent an activity to visitors than its original function of travel. When this occurs it is generally easiest to list the resource according to its most predominant function in terms of visitor use.

However, this inventory is not meant to be merely a basic checklist of attractions and services, but a structured listing of resources in terms of their type, capacity, market, operations, ownership and accessibility. It is no good knowing a resource exists if you do not know where to go or who to contact about its role or potential development for a tourism purpose. Therefore the second step in developing the inventory is to create a database of resources which indicates these points of ownership and operations, etc., which can be easily accessed and periodically updated as situations change.

Undoubtedly, the creation of such an inventory will lead to a very large data set for some destinations, which if not properly organized may prove of little use to the production of a development strategy. It is therefore essential that as the data is collected it is entered into a database, or tabulated in a concise format that will allow for easy retrieval and analysis. Examples of data charts for each of the five resource categories are presented in the Appendices at the end of this chapter.

Inventory of Natural Resources: list all those features of the environment which visitors might primarily like to see, or use for some activity. Key questions to consider in listing these features include:

♦ what makes this resource unique to the area?

♦ is it common or readily available in other destinations?

♦ how significant is it as an existing or potential attraction?

The information to be collected on each natural feature should include the following (see Appendix 4a):

> ♦ name and location from central point or tourist information centre;
> ♦ accessibility (restrictions, access points, disability); ownership and management;
> ♦ contact information;
> ♦ current volume of activity/level of use;
> ♦ visitor types (origin, activity, demographics);
> ♦ visitor services (toilets, parking).

Obviously this data cannot be collected for all natural resources, but wherever it is relevant it is useful to the evaluation of tourism potential later in the development process.

Inventory of Cultural Resources: list all those features of the built environment and cultural groups which visitors may like to see or learn more about. Key questions to consider in listing these resources should include:

♦ what makes the feature unique to the area?

♦ is there any social or cultural sensitivity?

♦ how significant is the resource as an existing or potential attraction?

The information to be collected on each cultural feature should include the following (see Appendix 4b):

> ♦ name and location from central point or tourist information centre;
> ♦ accessibility (restrictions, access points, disability);
> ♦ ownership and management (conservation, development or promotion);
> ♦ contact information;
> ♦ current volume of activity/level of use;
> ♦ season of operation;
> ♦ admission rates, if any;
> ♦ visitor types (origin, activity, demographics).

Inventory of Event Resources: this should list all those festivals and other event-type activities which are held in the destination on a regular or annual basis. This could also include less frequent activities, but as they may only be a one-off event they will be less significant to the tourism development strategy. In listing festivals and events it is generally advisable to set a minimum size criterion in terms of participants, so that those included will be large enough to draw people to the area. Key questions to consider in listing these resources include:

♦ what makes the event unique?

♦ does it attract non-local participants?

♦ does it complement or compete with other local events?

♦ what is the frequency of occurrence?

The type of information to be collected on each event should include the following (see Appendix 4c):

♦ name and location of event from central point or tourist information centre;
♦ timing (season and length of event);
♦ organization and management;
♦ contact information;
♦ number of participants and spectators (local vs. visitor);
♦ visitor types (origin, activity, demographics);
♦ types of participant activities;
♦ types of spectator activities;
♦ entry fees, if any.

<u>Inventory of Activity Resources:</u> list all facilities, purpose-built attractions, recreational amenities and other services which either directly serve a visitor market, or may serve a dual market of resident and tourist. Attractions tend to be those facilities which visitors pay to use; recreational amenities will include facilities which draw people in, but their use may not be the main reason for the visit; other services include opportunities for leisure shopping and general entertainment. Key questions to consider in listing these resources include:

♦ how unique is the 'activity' to the destination?

♦ does it attract non-local users?

The information to be collected on each activity should include the following (see Appendix 4d):

> ♦ name and location from central point or tourist information centre;
> ♦ timing and seasons of operation;
> ♦ accessibility (restrictions, access points, disability);
> ♦ ownership and management;
> ♦ contact information;
> ♦ current volume of activity/level of use;
> ♦ visitor types (origin, activity, demographics);
> ♦ user fees, admission rates, membership requirements.

Inventory of Service Resources: this can be potentially quite cumbersome as it includes various aspects of transport, accommodation, catering, hospitality and general community services. For a number of these subcategories, local directories and timetables may already exist and this exercise will just entail filling in a few extra details, including:

> ♦ name & location of service provider;
> ♦ contact information;
> ♦ description of general services.

While this information is important, it should always be collected in the context of its application to a tourism development strategy. That is, the types of services to be listed should play some role in providing, or potentially providing a service to visitors (see Appendix 4e). Much of this data can be used to create a basic local directory of service functions in the destination including travel and transport, retail, health and safety, financial and other general travel-related services.

In addition, for **accommodation services**, the data should also include the following (see Appendix 4f):

> ♦ name & location of facility from central point or tourist information centre;
> ♦ type and rating of facility;
> ♦ services offered (pool, catering, conference facilities);
> ♦ season of operation;
> ♦ accessibility issues (disability restrictions, types of users);

contd

- ◆ ownership and contact information;
- ◆ number of bed spaces/basic volume;
- ◆ level of use;
- ◆ visitor types (origin, activity, demographics);
- ◆ rates and fees.

For **catering services**, the data should also include the following (see Appendix 4g):

- ◆ name & location of facility from central point or tourist information centre;
- ◆ type and rating of facility (fast-food, family, fine dining, etc.);
- ◆ accessibility issues (disability restrictions);
- ◆ ownership and contact information;
- ◆ seating capacity and hours of operation;
- ◆ level of use and user types (demographics);
- ◆ average meal costs/set menu prices.

For **reception services** the data should relate to all services and facilities available from each visitor information centre or service point, and include the following (see Appendix 4h):

- ◆ name and location of information service;
- ◆ hours of operation (if applicable);
- ◆ services available (language, guiding, souvenir sales);
- ◆ information available (leaflets, maps, etc.);
- ◆ contact information;
- ◆ current volume of activity/level of use;
- ◆ visitor types (origin, activity, demographics).

It is also important to indicate the location of static information points and displays, interpretation boards, and road and pedestrian signposting which are relevant to visitor activity. It may be easiest to list these elements by indicating them with specific symbols on a *tourism base-map* of the destination. The creation of such a map is also very useful to:

- ◆ identify the physical location of natural and cultural resources;
- ◆ indicate where to find various activity resources, particularly when they rely on the use of natural or cultural resources;
- ◆ to indicate the physical location of different services such as accommodation, catering and other key service providers.

In addition, event resources can be marked on a map to indicate where they take place, while at the same time it is also very useful to develop an annual calendar of events, giving an overview of when certain festivals and other activities will take place. This will not only aid in the build-up and preparation for events, but gives a relatively instant picture of what is taking place to attract visitors and where there may be gaps in which to develop other tourism events (see Appendix 4j). However, all of these resources should still be listed in tabular form, and included in some form of local directory of all tourism activities, services and events.

One point relevant to the inventory of all resource types concerns the collection of data in terms of actual visitor use (see Chapter 5), including:

♦ who uses the resource;
♦ when they do so;
♦ in what numbers;
♦ for what purpose.

This type of visitor data is vital in understanding the link between supply and demand, particularly when it comes to assessing the 'value added' to a destination by new development activity, the effectiveness of marketing campaigns, or the general structure of tourism demand. Understandably, some facilities or commercial ventures will be concerned about the release of such data in terms of competition and data confidence, but if this can be collected sensitively with certain restrictions on use, then this issue need not be of concern. However, without this type of market intelligence it can be very difficult for a destination effectively to monitor its activities and improve its tourism services (see Chapter 9).

STAGE 2 – Resource Evaluation

While the first stage of the audit should have identified what a place has to offer, the second stage is designed to help further develop a general picture of where the destination broadly fits within the wider tourism marketplace. Once the inventory is complete, the evaluation stage is meant to identify what is good about these resources and working well, and what aspects are in need of further attention, or where improvements need to be made if the destination is to compete successfully.

Although most communities or regions have many basic tourism resources, it is not good enough to simply count or list these, because their quality may be below standard, or offer exactly the same experience as anywhere else. Each resource feature should be evaluated in turn on the basis of their overall *quality*, *uniqueness* and *appeal*, and then summarized in terms of an overall evaluation of the resource in relation to its role in the future development of the destination's tourism industry (see Appendix Figure 4j).

Resource Quality: Tourism is an industry driven by consumer demand but one which effectively sells an intangible product. We cannot touch it, take it home or try it out for a few days to see if we like it. Nor can we return it if we are not satisfied. Tourism sells an experience, and the quality of that experience is becoming ever more important as tourists increasingly seek and expect better value for money from tourism products.

However, resource quality is not just about customer service (see Chapter 8), it includes conservation and management as well. It is overall quality which is vital to the continued success and development of the industry in any location. For example, while a destination may have a lovely riverside setting as a key natural resource, if access to the river is severally restricted, if there are limitations on the use of moorings or landing stages, or parts of the river are unnavigable, the quality of the resource as it concerns tourism may be questionable. The river may very well be a significant feature, but the constraints on its use may serve to limit its value as a key factor in tourism development.

Questions to think about when assessing '*quality*' include:

♦ what makes this resource better or worse than somewhere else?

♦ what are its weak points, or where is it vulnerable?

♦ is it well maintained?

♦ is quality of service consistent throughout?

♦ how might the resource be improved?

♦ what are the main drawbacks to further development?

Resource Uniqueness: Generally, the less unique a destination or the weaker its sense of place, the harder it will be both to draw people in and compete in the tourism marketplace. Indeed, if every tourism destination offered virtually the same set of attractions, shops, restaurants, environment and quality of service, tourism would become somewhat meaningless.

With ever-increasing competition, the more successful destinations will be those which build upon resources that help separate them out from all the others. Just copying what others have done will not mean success, and could even be counterproductive if the quality of the copy is not exceptionally better than the original.

However, almost all destinations have something about them which can be used to help establish this sense of place. This may focus on one or more of the resource categories, and is based on the character of the resource in that particular setting. While it may not be possible to identify something that is unique, what gives the destination its sense of place is how the resource has been used or developed in that particular setting. Even when the resource base is very similar to other competing destinations, there is always an opportunity to identify aspects which are different and which can help create that separate and unique identity. The inventory stage should help highlight a number of features which can be exploited to this end.

As with resource quality, examine the uniqueness of the resource by thinking how each feature might be used to highlight the differences between similar tourist destinations. Key questions to think about when assessing uniqueness include:

♦ what is special about the resource in this particular setting?

♦ what makes it different from somewhere else?

♦ how does the resource reflect a sense of place?

Resource Appeal: The third element in evaluation is to consider the tourism appeal or drawing power of each resource feature. When evaluating appeal, it is useful to consider each feature in terms of how it fits within the current catalogue of tourism activities, and where there may be opportunities to develop this further. Key questions to think about when considering appeal include:

♦ what role does it play in current visitor activity (principal or supporting)?

♦ how is visitor use measured or assessed?

♦ how could the resource be made more appealing?

Although tourism appeal is often measured simply by data concerning visitor use (i.e. volume, origin, etc.), this can be misleading because this does not necessarily give a true indication of real drawing power. Almost all resource features play some role in attracting visitors to the destination, but some are clearly more important than others. Indeed, just because a tourist visits a number of different attractions in a destination this does not mean those features had anything to do with the initial drawing power of the place. In fact what may represent a central feature of a destination may not in itself actually play a major role in drawing people to the place. Rather it is often the use which is made of that resource which represents the real tourism appeal. For example, a river or lake may be considered a core attraction in some destinations, but without the opportunity to utilize this resource for some tourism activity, the practical drawing power may be reduced.

WHAT TO DO NEXT?

The core function of the *tourism resource audit* is to create a database of tourism resources and provide an overall assessment of those features in terms of their development opportunities and constraints. When the audit is complete the following questions should be easily and comprehensively answered:

♦ what makes a resource feature an asset or potential benefit to the destination, i.e. what makes it good?

♦ what aspects of tourism are currently adequate or satisfactory, but which will need some attention if they are to play a more central role in future development?

♦ what, if any, are the negative aspects of the resource in question which may need improving or changing (e.g. the Tourist Information Centre is closed on Sundays)?

♦ what, if any, aspects of the destination represent a potential disadvantage to the further development of tourism (e.g. deforestation has increased the likelihood of flooding and landslip in the area)?

Overall, the audit is meant to identify what is good about tourism from a supply point of view, and what areas or aspects may need improvement. In doing so it will also help indicate key opportunities for tourism growth, and areas of concern or constraints which will need to be addressed during the production of a tourism development strategy (see Chapter 6). However, though the audit essentially examines tourism supply, this is only one-half of the equation. If destinations are to be successful, they need to attract visitors who are going to use the various resources on offer. But not all visitors are interested in all destinations, nor are all visitors interested in all resources which may be available to them in any one location. Attempting to attract all types of visitors will not guarantee anything and may in fact prove counterproductive.

Successful tourism development, therefore, not only depends on a clear understanding of how resources fit together, but on attracting the types of tourists who will most likely use them and so create the greatest benefit for the destination. However, not all tourists have the same impact, depending on their length of stay, interests and spending power, etc. (see Chapter 2). The next stage in the tourism development process is therefore to identify those groups of visitors who already come to the destination, which of these create the greatest benefit and then to consider potential markets they could also be encouraged to visit. This is the essence of understanding tourism demand, which is the subject of Chapter 5.

FURTHER READING *for Understanding Tourism Resources*

Getz, D. (1991) *Festivals, Special Events and Tourism*. New York: Van Nostrand Reinhold.

Gunn, C. (1994) *Tourism Planning: basics, concepts, cases* (3rd edition). Bristol: PA., Taylor & Francis.

Middleton, V.T.C. (1994) 'The Tourist Product', in Witt, S.F. and Moutinho, L. (eds) *Tourism Marketing and Management Handbook* (2nd edition). Hemel Hempstead: Prentice Hall International.

Smith, S. (1989) *Tourism Analysis*. New York: Longman Scientific & Technical.

Appendix 4a

Inventory of Natural Resources

NATURAL	Name of feature (and managers)	Location (map reference)	Accessibility	Users (m/e)[1]	Visitor services	Visitor data[2]	Contact (name and telephone)
LANDSCAPE							
FLORA							
FAUNA							
WATER							

1 users: level of activity/current user numbers – m=measured, e=estimated   2 visitor data: collected or uncollected

Appendix 4b

Inventory of Cultural Resources

CULTURAL	Name of feature (and managers)	Location (map reference)	Access	Opening times	Users (m/e)[1]	Admission fees	Visitor data[2]	Contact (name and telephone)
HERITAGE								
RELIGIOUS								
OTHER CULTURAL								

1 users: level of activity/current user numbers – m=measured, e=estimated   2 visitor data: collected or uncollected

Appendix 4c

Inventory of Event Resources

EVENTS	Name of event (and managers)	Location (map reference)	Dates	Type of activities	Patronage (m/e)[1]	Visitor data[2]	Contact (name and telephone)
FESTIVALS							
TOURNAMENTS							
BUSINESS EVENTS							
OTHER EVENTS							

1 patronage: number of visitors – m=measured, e=estimated   2 visitor data: collected or uncollected

Appendix 4d

Inventory of Activity Resources

ACTIVITY	Name of resource	Location (map reference)	Opening times	Seasonal restrictions	User fees	Visitor data[1]	Contact (name and telephone)
RECREATIONAL							
SERVICES							
FACILITIES							

1 visitor data: collected or uncollected

Appendix 4e

Sample Items of Basic Service Directory

Accommodation	Book shops	Delicatessens	Gift stores	Locksmiths	Shoe sales and repair

Accommodation
  hotels
  B&B
Antique dealers
Aquariums
Baby sitting/child care
Bakers
Banks
Bicycles
  rental
  sales and service
Blacksmiths
Boat
  rental
  sales and service

Book shops
Butchers
Bus and coach services
Camera sales and service
Camping and caravan sites
Car
  rental
  sales and service
Clothes store
  ladies' wear
  men's wear
  children's wear
Churches
Cinemas
Convenience stores

Delicatessens
Department stores
Doctor's office/surgery
Dry cleaners
Electrical sales and service
Foreign exchange
Fishing supplies
Florists
Grocers
  fruit and vegetable
  supermarkets
Gas appliance sales and
  service

Gift stores
  arts and craft
  china and glass
  greetings cards
  souvenirs
Golf-courses
Gym (fitness)
Hairdressers
Hardware and household
  supplies
Hospitals
  casualty/ER
Jewellers
Libraries
Local government

Locksmiths
Motor-cycle sales and service
Museums
Newsagents
Off-licence
Pet supplies
Petrol stations
Police
Post office
Pubs/wine bars
Record/CD sales
Restaurants
  cafés
  full service
  takeaway

Shoe sales and repair
Societies and clubs
Solicitors
Sporting goods
Sports facilities
Taxi services
Tourist information centres
Translators
Veterinary services
Video rental

Appendix 4f

Inventory of Accommodation Services

ACCOMMODATION	Name	Location (map reference)	Classification	Beds/units/sites	Room rates	Services*:
HOTELS						
GUEST-HOUSES						
B&B						
CAMPING						

*1: Outdoor swimming-pool, 2: Indoor swimming-pool, 3: Hottub/whirlpool/jacuzzi, 4: Sauna, 5: Games room, 6: Gym, 7: Tennis-courts, 8: Air-conditioning, 9: Café, 10: Restaurant, 11: Lounge, 12: Pub/bar, 13: Conference facilities, 14: Disabled access, 15: Self-catering facilities, 16: Souvenir sales, 17: Food store, 18: Power, 19: Water, 20: Sani-station, 21: Firewood

Appendix 4g

Inventory of Catering Resources

CATERING	Name	Location (map reference)	Food type	Seating capacity	Entrée costs	Opening hours
FULL-SERVICE RESTAURANTS						
FAMILY RESTAURANTS						
CAFÉS						
TAKEAWAY						

Appendix 4h

Inventory of Reception Services

RECEPTION	Location	Contact (name & tel.)	Opening times	Publications/ Guide Books (last updated)	Maps (last updated)	Attraction Leaflets (last updated)	Languages Spoken	Souvenir Items
Main Information Centre								
Secondary Information Centre								
Information Point A								
Information Point B								
Information Point C								

Appendix 4i

Annual Calendar of Tourism Events

TOURISM EVENT	JAN	FEB	MAR	APR	MAY	JUN	JUL	AUG	SEPT	OCT	NOV	DEC	JAN

Appendix 4j

Resource Evaluation

Resource feature	Quality issues	Relative uniqueness	Appeal – drawing power
NATURAL			
CULTURAL			
EVENTS			
ACTIVITIES			
SERVICES			

CHAPTER FIVE

Who do we want?
Selecting the tourist

INTRODUCTION

Tourism destinations need actively to manage their visitors in order to ensure their long-term success. This requires knowledge about who the tourists actually are – based on information that goes beyond casual observation. Tourists are not a homogeneous mass – far from it; individuals can show a wide range of differences relevant to tourism management and sustainability. Knowing which groups sharing similar characteristics would bring greatest benefit and minimal cost to the destination, both now and in the future, is the skill that forms the focus of this chapter. Indeed, identifying and selecting groups, or segments, of tourists that a destination can satisfy, preferably better than competitors, is central to any marketing practice (see Chapter 7).

Demand for tourism is constantly changing, so information on tourist characteristics needs to be gathered on a continuous basis. The destination that fails to notice trends and to take a series of decisions on attractive tourist groups, will generally find that, through time, the types of tourists arriving become less and less advantageous to the area. This holds true even for popular destinations, who find that numbers swell dramatically even as the desirability of the tourist profile dwindles. Likewise, destinations who only examine their current tourists, rather than also exploring the potential market, are liable to find themselves in a similar trap. All lead to a weaker position against better managed competitors. Table 5.1 (on page 90) indicates some of the qualitative trends influencing the demand for tourism. As the table highlights, tourists from the established tourist-generating countries, such as the United Kingdom, Germany or the United States, are increasingly experienced as travellers and, consequently, more demanding in what they expect to get for their money.

By the year 2020, there will be 1.6 billion international tourist arrivals worldwide, generating over US$2 trillion, i.e. annual growth rates of 4.3% and 6.7% respectively. Domestic tourism will outnumber international arrivals by 10:1 (World Tourism Organization, 1997: 3–4)

Fixed ➡ Flexible
Search for bespoke products, tailor-made packages and maximum flexibility.

Careless ➡ Concerned
Increasing recognition of negative impacts and demand for a quality environment.

Escape ➡ Extension of life
Search for authentic or spontaneous experiences, learning and communication with others.

Sun ➡ Nature
Search for safe sun plus additional nature-based activities.

Passive ➡ Active
Mental and physical exertion, new skill acquisition, or update existing interests. Products based on entertainment, excitement or education, or some combination.

Naïve ➡ Experienced
Tourist as experienced and demanding consumer, unfazed by novelty and in pursuit of individuality.

Single ➡ Mixed
Tendency to mix destination product elements from different price categories, e.g. budget transport, luxury accommodation, etc.

Slow ➡ Fast
Less regulation and restriction on global travel, harmonization of currencies, use of technology to speed up travel process and distribution of travel products.

Time-pressured ➡ Time-crunched
Increasingly, consumers in the urbanized developed world are stretched for time. They balance many tasks and roles and live in a 24-hour society where services are increasingly available around the clock. Standards for tourism are compared against other services, and organizing vacations becomes another list of tasks to be stacked.

Price-based ➡ Image-based
Image critical to ability of destination to attract tourists. Tourists using destinations as branded fashion accessories to help identify themselves from the mass of tourists and to make statements about themselves to others.

Table 5.1: Future Trends Influencing Demand for Tourism
(Adapted from World Tourism Organization, 1991, 1997; Poon, 1993; Laine, 1989)

Any local destination competing for tourists is operating in a challenging global environment, even if individual local businesses might struggle to recognize this. A competitive position can only be developed and maintained if sound decisions are made on the groups of tourists best suited to the destination. For example, the family market is less susceptible to the growth of long-haul destinations than other tourist groups, and therefore may form the core market for a destination located close to large tourist-generating regions. According to the World Tourism Organization (1997), the future holds opportunities for both large-scale or mainstream tourism and for small-scale niche tourism. The key lies with finding the groups of tourists that best match the abilities and capacities of the individual destination.

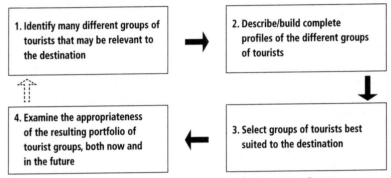

Figure 5.1: Who Do We Want? Stages in the Decision Process

Figure 5.1 refers to the different stages in the process of identifying, describing and selecting groups of tourists for a local destination. It acts as a simple guide to the layout of this chapter.

IDENTIFYING AND DESCRIBING GROUPS OF TOURISTS

To break down the mass of tourists into groups, or alternatively to build up individual tourists into workable segments, a number of descriptors or variables may be used. There is a wide range of options available; the art is in selecting those of most relevance. Universally applicable, however, is a broad breakdown by:

♦ tourists (staying visitors) and same-day visitors;

♦ domestic and international visitors;

♦ purpose of travel broadly defined as leisure, business, and visiting friends and relatives (VFR);

♦ package-tour and independent visitors.

All four are useful starting-points for identifying groups of visitors that might be of interest to a destination. Much attention is given to international visitors at the expense of the domestic market, which is too often neglected. In fact, a strong domestic market can provide a lower risk and solid base for gradual tourism development, allowing for eventual expansion into the international market as the product improves. The number of tourists (with the possible exception of VFR) is determined by the bed capacity of the accommodation at the destination. As staying visitors tend to generate greater income for the locality, increasing the length of stay becomes a priority for many destinations. Day-visitors are often overlooked. Tourists tend to be associated with holiday travel, yet conferences, sales trips, meetings and incentive travel as a company reward for achievement, are all growth areas, albeit competitive ones. Destinations often forget to examine VFR tourists, partly because the accommodation element of the stay is less visible. But VFR segments are characterized by emotional bonds to the area, and may be more resilient than other tourist segments

Check points	%	Satisfactory balance? yes / no?	Potential to increase? yes / no?
Tourists (staying)			
Same-day visitors			
	100		
Domestic visitors			
International visitors			
	100		
Leisure tourists			
Business tourists			
VFR tourists			
	100		
Package tourists			
Independent tourists			
	100		

Table 5.2: Check Points for Categorizing Current Tourist Groups

to negative incidents or economic downturn. Historical roots to a destination may be exploited two or three generations later as people wish to learn something about their ancestors. Such tourist groups may be of particular relevance to a destination that has experienced substantial out-migration of its inhabitants in the past, and it may be relatively easy to locate such people through industry associations or societies.

Although there is a blur between the package and the independent tourist, the distinction is important to a destination choosing tourist segments to target. After the initial decision, a package tourist has placed many trip decisions in the hands of the holiday or excursion company. Attracting package tourists makes it crucially important that the destination builds strong links with the package provider, whether they are coach, ferry or incoming tour operators. Ideally, such organizations should be carefully selected, with a view to building a long-term relationship. Destinations should be aware of the potential shift in the balance of power if tourists are chosen through this method; benefits may flow back to the organizer rather than to the destination, and operators may pull out of an area at short notice. Most tour operators have slim profit margins, which makes them tough negotiators with accommodation and transport suppliers because they are constantly fighting to control costs. Independent tourists maintain flexibility and control in decision-making and are more open to increasing their length of stay, visiting attractions, etc. Table 5.2 summarizes the four grouping possibilities for any local destination.

Having established these four very broad categories, other variables may then be used. For simplicity, the variables fall under two main headings:

♦ **trip variables** or variables that relate the person to the tourism experience in some way; see Table 5.3;

♦ **personal variables** or variables that relate solely to the person involved, distinct from the tourism experience itself; see Table 5.4.

Tables 5.3 and 5.4 illustrate some of the variables under these two headings; those highlighted are drawn out as discussion points below. Generally, these tables represent a useful starting-point in the process of selecting key visitor markets which a destination may seek to attract.

Discussion Points for Trip Variables

The following are all discussion points arising from Table 5.3, which examines trip variables that may be used in creating groups of tourists.

Trip Variables

❑ Purpose of travel, e.g. leisure/business/VFR
❑ **Benefits sought by tourist**
❑ Expectations of standards for trip, e.g. as at home? lower? higher?
❑ **Distance living from destination**
❑ **Spend per head/day/trip**
❑ **Spend by component, e.g. accommodation, shopping, etc.**
❑ **Price sensitivity**
❑ Other marketing factor sensitivity, e.g. to sales promotions, to advertising
❑ Method of payment, e.g. cash, credit card, convertible currency, etc.
❑ Timing of payment, e.g. how far in advance, during, after?
❑ Attitude towards destination, e.g. enthusiastic, positive, indifferent, negative, hostile
❑ Buyer readiness stage, e.g. unaware of destination, aware, informed, interested, purchase intention
❑ Usage status, e.g. non-, ex-, first, regular user, etc.
❑ Usage rate, e.g. heavy, medium, light
❑ Frequency of use, e.g. once a year, twice a year
❑ **Purchase roles**, e.g. who makes the decision? joint? who influences? children? who pays?
❑ Purchase occasion, e.g. honeymoon, religious celebration, birthday, etc.
❑ **Timing of booking**, e.g. how far in advance, days/weeks/months, last minute, on spec
❑ Timing of trip, e.g. month, peak, shoulder, trough
❑ Use of travel organizers, e.g. airlines, tour operators, travel agents, ferry operators, car hire, etc.
❑ **Sources of information used**, e.g. word of mouth, brochures, web sites, newspapers, etc.
❑ Method of booking, e.g. direct, TIC, third-party, etc.
❑ **Point of capture**, e.g. origin country, gateway airport or city, en route, etc.
❑ Mode of transport used to arrive/once arrived, e.g. car, ferry, bicycle, airplane, etc.
❑ Attractions/accommodation/activities/facilities used and pattern of use
❑ Trip patterns, e.g. touring, stop-over, single destination, twin destinations, etc.
❑ Party size by adult/children
❑ Party composition, e.g. adults, children, friends, families, relations, etc.
❑ Length of stay, e.g. hours, nights
❑ Sensitivity and awareness of cultural, social and environmental aspects of the destination. Extent of cultural gap between hosts and visitors?
❑ Satisfaction levels, e.g. unsatisfied, very satisfied, etc.

Table 5.3: Trip Variables Used for Describing Groups of Tourists

♦ The distance that the potential tourist or day-visitor lives from the destination will determine the likely demand catchment area. The analysis of the components of the destination will suggest its pulling force, be it local urban areas, regional, national, cross-border international, short-haul international, or long-haul international. It may be more informative to measure distance in terms of:

(a) cost/expense to the individual tourist,
(b) time taken to reach the destination, and
(c) effort required and complexity of journey arrangements.

♦ Often destinations focus on the number of trips or tourists as a target, rather than on the beneficial variables of *spend per head/day/trip* and the percentage of this figure that is retained and circulated round the local economy. As a general rule, where the transport costs of getting to and from the destination represent a high percentage of the total holiday cost, the tourist is less inclined to be sensitive to individual cost issues at the destination itself. The groups of tourists who exhibit high spend per head/day/trip, travel frequently and show destination loyalty are desirable segments. However, the advantages they bring are recognized by established destinations, and competition for these segments can be intense.

♦ Purchasing a tourism experience is a complex procedure. Classic marketing theory points to a variety of *buying roles*, such as the *initiator* of the idea, the *information gatherer*, the *influencer*, the *decider*, the *buyer* and the *final user*. Tourism is often undertaken as a group experience, whether with family or friends, with any group member taking on one or more of the buying roles. The same holds true for business tourism, where, typically, the buyer and even the decider may not be the same person as the user. Business tourism is also quite likely to include a specific role responsible for filtering and screening information.

♦ As a local destination has limited financial resources, it may be easier to *capture* the independent tourist once they have entered the country, rather than at the tourist's home country. Table 5.5 suggests possible ways of attracting the tourist at trip points other than the home country. Repeat visitors to the destination country may be more receptive to such approaches than the first-time visitor.

♦ The *benefits* sought by the tourist are an essential variable in examining groups of tourists. A sound understanding of desired benefits will guide a better fit between the destination assets and groups of tourists that the destination is best able to satisfy. Table 5.6 illustrates a range of benefits that can be sought by tourists. Typically, tourists are seeking a cluster of benefits from any tourism experience, rather than a single benefit alone. A hierarchy of benefits within the cluster may be evident. Some of the benefits may be described as *push factors*, as they are more concerned with conditions at the origin than at the destination. Others may be described as *pull factors* as they are more positively associated with attraction towards the specific destination.

♦ Trip variables can be subdivided into pre-trip variables, during-trip variables and post-trip variables. For the tourist, the tourism experience begins with anticipation and finishes with memories. Too often, local destinations only consider the stay itself as the experience, forgetting to include the journeys to and away from the area as part of the tourist's experience.

♦ Tourism is a high-risk purchase. The financial cost is high and precious leisure time lost on a poor vacation choice cannot be reclaimed. Thus tourists may show anxiety in the period *between making the purchase* and *starting the trip*, a length of time that could span several days to several months. Letters or promotional print, emphasizing the soundness of choice, perhaps using testimonials from relevant personalities or satisfied tourists, can act to reassure or to allay fears.

As a high-risk purchase, potential tourists tend to value informal *sources of information* from friends and family above formal information sources from a destination which they may perceive as biased. There are usually individuals, or opinion leaders, who are believed by their associates to be experts on particular topics. Their advice will be influential on the purchase decision. Identifying the opinion leaders for different groups of tourists can help positive word-of-mouth recommendation, which is critical to destination success. Opinion leaders are likely to be frequent users of travel and tourism products and to be amongst the first of a certain tourist type to visit a particular destination.

Discussion Points for Personal Variables
The following are all discussion points arising from Table 5.4, which examines personal variables that may be used in creating groups of tourists.

Personal Variables

- ❏ Gender male / female
- ❏ Marital status
- ❏ Age
- ❏ **Nationality / country of residence**
- ❏ Ethnic origin
- ❏ Education level attained, e.g. school, university, etc.
- ❏ Religion, e.g. Muslim, Christian, Jewish, etc.
- ❏ Occupation, e.g. manual, professional, self-employed, etc.
- ❏ Income (and income after paying for life necessities)
- ❏ Household size, e.g. single, couple, etc.
- ❏ Household composition, e.g. birth families, step-families, extended families, single parents, friends, etc.
- ❏ Social class (scheme varies by nationality)
- ❏ Population density, e.g. rural, urban, suburban, low density, high density
- ❏ Climatic conditions of home area
- ❏ Currency received as wages / salary (exchange rates)
- ❏ **Geodemographic tools** (where feasible)
- ❏ Media habits, e.g. TV usage, radio, newspapers, magazines, web sites, etc.
- ❏ Car ownership
- ❏ Holiday leave entitlement and structure (varies by nationality), e.g. national holidays, school year, long weekends, number of days' leave and pattern of use, etc.
- ❏ Previous travel experience
- ❏ Lifestyle and attitudes, interest, opinions and hobbies
- ❏ Lifestage, e.g. single, couple, with children, younger/older, mature couples, retired, solitary survivor, etc.

Table 5.4: Personal Variables for Describing Groups of Tourists

♦ Given financial constraints, *nationality* (or *country of residence*) is a useful starting-point for destinations. National tourist organizations typically select major country markets or growth countries in which to concentrate their promotional resources. Often they can only afford to have a tourist office or representative in key countries. It is useful for a local destination to know the pattern of overseas offices and representatives maintained by their national tourist organizations as this is likely to reflect the pattern of opportunities and help available for promotional and distribution activities.

♦ *Geodemographic* tools which combine computerized information systems with government census data show groups of people sharing similar characteristics identified by their postcode, zipcode or street. In the United Kingdom, tools such as ACORN (*A Classification of Residential Neighbourhoods*), Mosaic and

PinPoint are all available at a price. Availability of such geodemographic tools will vary by country; however, they may be too costly for a local destination to consider unless a financial partner or subsidy is found.

Of course, not all the variables will be appropriate at any one time. The idea is to mix and match, to build possible groups of tourists for the destination to focus on for marketing activity. If this is done creatively, new and exciting groups of tourists may emerge that have not already been spotted by competitors. As a generalization, the trip variables are most useful in forming the skeleton of characteristics, while the personal variables are most useful in adding flesh to the bones. In other words:

♦ firstly, use variables to identify groups of tourists that can be differentiated from other groups of tourists (often using trip variables, but not exclusively). As few as two or three variables may be sufficient for this;

♦ secondly, use other variables to build a complete picture of each tourist group (often using personal variables, but not exclusively). The description should be as detailed as possible and should incorporate media habits.

Used together, a complete profile of any tourist group can be assembled. The aim at this stage is to produce descriptions of a range of possible tourist groups for the destination without considering their relative merits. To achieve this, think about using:

♦ computer databases of visitor characteristics and computerized techniques for survey analysis where available (usually only national tourist organizations have sufficient resources to conduct such analysis);

♦ the experience of any tourism businesses currently operating in the area or adjacent areas regarding the types of tourists they currently attract and hope to attract (a bottom-up approach);

♦ any information released by the government, national tourist office, regional equivalents, tourist information centres (TICs) and other relevant bodies. Apart from one-off studies where more detail will be given, such published information at a national level typically includes number of trips/visitors, number of nights, length of stay, spend per head/trip, tourist nationality, accommodation used, purpose of travel and the month during which the trip was taken (see Chapter 9). Understanding the national trends for incoming tourism helps the local destination to establish a framework of possibilities that reflects patterns at a larger scale, useful knowledge when resources are limited;

♦ teams composed of people with varying perspectives (see Chapter 3);

♦ analysis of competitors' brochures, advertisements, videos and promotional print.

Once the tourist group options are assembled, the destination can move on to select specific segments to target.

Point of capture: En route / during journey to destination country **Possible methods**: Inflight/ferry magazine (article/advert), inflight/ferry video (by national tourist organization), promotional print at airport, ferry terminal, rail/coach station, car hire, petrol stations on key roads.
Point of capture: Capital city/gateway city **Possible methods**: Promotional print at TICs, transport stations, travel agencies, car-hire outlets, accommodation enterprises from hotels to bed and breakfast, attractions (especially gift shops).
Point of capture: Touring **Possible methods**: As above, along identified circuits and routes used by particular groups of independent tourists. Promotional print held by car breakdown services, garages, local police as appropriate.

Table 5.5: Point of Tourist Capture

Benefit sought by leisure tourist	
❏ Rest & relaxation	❏ Revive/repair relationships
❏ Recovery, recuperation, regeneration	❏ Search for love or sex
❏ Inner peace & tranquillity	❏ Broaden the mind/education
❏ Escape/get away from routine	❏ Learn/improve skills or interests
❏ Fitness/health	❏ Freedom & self-determination
❏ Pursuit of youth/beauty myth	❏ Play/release of adult tension
❏ Social contact/belonging	❏ Status & prestige

Table 5.6: Benefits Sought by Leisure Tourists from Destinations

SELECTING GROUPS OF TOURISTS

Having experimented with different personal variables and trip variables and then built profiles of the resulting tourist groups, decisions are needed as to the most suitable tourist segments for the destination to target. Of course, few local destinations start this exercise with a blank sheet of paper, as there are likely to be existing groups of tourists that have evolved through time. However, decisions are required:

♦ to protect the medium- and long-term future of the local destination;

♦ to make the most effective and efficient use of limited financial resources;

♦ so that opportunities for potential new tourist segments are not overlooked.

In addition, destructive segments can be deselected, with a view to discouraging their arrival through demarketing, a reversal of the common role of segmentation as stated above. This section explores the criteria and issues involved with (a) choosing tourist segments and (b) ensuring a sound collection or portfolio of tourist segments.

Choosing Tourist Groups

Ideally, a tourist segment should show as little variation in characteristics between group members as possible. Similarity is the key. In practice, subgroups, or micro-segments, may be identified, and, if financially viable, these eventually may form segments to be targeted in their own right. The criteria to be used in choosing tourist groups are best agreed by the local destination concerned. Possible tourist segments should be systematically scored against the criteria to form a solid base for informed discussion (see Table 5.7).

Criteria	Weighting (if applicable)	Tourist group a	Tourist group b	Tourist group c	etc.
Criterion A	x 2.0	2 / 4			
Criterion B	x 1.5	2 / 3			
Criterion C	x 0.5	4 / 2			
etc.					
Total score		8 / 9			

Table 5.7: Scoring Tourist Groups   Scoring scale of 0–5 (minimum = 1, maximum = 5)

Similar tables can be drawn up for competitors and the results compared. However the table is used, the following questions should be considered for inclusion on the list of criteria.

♦ Will the tourist segment help the destination to achieve its objectives? In the short term, perhaps as a stopgap measure? In the medium term? Perhaps even in the long term?

♦ Is the tourist segment appropriate to the destination? Does the group fit with the assets and pulling power of the destination? Table 5.8 outlines a grid that can be used to assess the attraction of assets against the different tourist groups. Is the tourist group's behaviour consistent with sustainability goals? How do the negative socio-cultural, economic and physical impacts of the group balance against the positive impacts of the group?

Resource/asset	Tourist Group				
	a	b	c	d	etc.
A	2/**4**				
B	4/**4**				
C	3/**1**				
etc.					
Total score	9/**9**				

Scoring scale 0–5 (minimum = 1, maximum = 5): Groups attraction/asset: Resource/asset's ability to absorb group
Italics = group's attraction to resource/asset; **Bold = resource/asset's ability to absorb group**

Table 5.8: Scoring Tourist Groups Against Destination Assets and Resources

♦ Can the tourist segment be measured? It is easier to manage objectives if tourist groups are amenable to monitoring and quantification.

♦ Can the tourist segment be reached through promotion? Some groups are hard to separate from the rest of the population. A clear profile of the tourist groups' media habits (see Table 5.4) and/or a characteristic applicable for direct mail is desirable to ensure the efficient use of the communications budget.

♦ Are the opinion leaders for the tourist segment easy to identify? Can they be reached with promotion? Given the prominence of word-of-mouth recommendation in purchasing tourism, this is an advantage.

♦ What is the size of the tourist segment? A small niche group that is growing and exhibits a high per trip spend can be financially attractive, but, in general, a large pool of potential tourists is a stronger starting-point.

♦ How financially viable is the tourist segment? It may not be financially viable in the short term, but must become viable in the medium to long term to justify resource allocation.

♦ How stable is the tourist segment? In the short term? In the medium term? Is the group growing or declining? If so, at what rate is it growing or declining? Destinations should be wary of entering declining markets.

♦ What is the risk associated with the tourist segment? How will the tourist group react to adverse exchange rates? Or to negative events that may occur, such as terrorism or flooding? Obviously, a resilient group is more attractive to a destination.

♦ Are competitors actively pursuing the same tourist segment? If so, does the competitor hold a strong advantage over the destination in attracting this group? Does the competitor have any weaknesses concerning this tourist group that could be exploited? Might there be benefits in joining forces and co-operating with one another in serving this group of tourists?

As a number of tourist segments will be selected, the destination also needs to consider how the different groups fit together as a portfolio.

Ensuring a Sound Portfolio of Tourist Groups

A local destination needs to choose a number of tourist segments, because a single segment focus would leave the destination vulnerable to change and to unforeseen events. It needs to develop a collection or portfolio of tourists, and to plan for its future development as changes occur in the external environment. Initial considerations for designing a strong portfolio of tourist segments include:

♦ Will the collection allow the destination to meet its goals and objectives? In the short, medium and long term?

♦ How many tourist segments should be selected? Too few and the destination is exposed to sudden downturns in a particular market; too many and the destination spreads its communications budget too thinly to achieve its objectives. A common platform for all/most of the tourist groups minimizes the duplication of marketing effort and allows the marketing budget to be used effectively.

♦ How compatible are the different tourist segments with one another? Remember that unless different tourist groups are separated either spatially or by time of year, they will influence the experience and satisfaction of other groups. Over the longer term, they will also influence the image of the destination. If tourist groups do not complement each other, then dissatisfaction and negative word of mouth can occur. Alternatively, separate out the groups so that they are visiting the destination at different times of the year or are using different parts of the destination.

♦ Examine the overall structure of the portfolio. How many segments are in a growing market, a declining market or a stable or mature market? In short, does the portfolio look balanced? At the current time? But what about in five years' time? If the future scenario is not acceptable, what tourist groups should be developed, maintained or eliminated so that a better balance is achieved?

♦ Is the destination over-reliant on any one or two segments? With reference to numbers or spend per head/day/trip? What action is required to reduce the problem?

♦ How resilient is the portfolio to disruption by external events, such as political activities or natural disasters? Of course, extreme events can stop tourism altogether, but relatively minor incidents can also have a negative effect and some groups, such as domestic tourists, may prove to be less adversely affected. What about the length of recovery time following a negative event?

♦ What does the portfolio look like when tourist segments are examined by time or month of use? Assuming that the objectives highlight year-round tourism, are the trough and shoulder months given sufficient attention? Generally speaking, year-round tourism is healthier for local businesses.

♦ Does the portfolio of tourist segments offer enough flexibility to individual providers of tourism at the destination? The framework should give ample opportunity for the different businesses to develop.

♦ How realistic is the portfolio in the context of the national framework? It is better to work with the national tourist organizations. Unless the local destination is based on outstanding resources of international recognition, it is more effective to fit the local portfolio into the national picture.

Table 5.9 presents a grid for completion to outline the portfolio of segments belonging to a local destination. Of course, a destination cannot control its boundaries (unless it is an inclusive resort), and is likely to be visited by tourist types outside of the preferred portfolio. These groups still need to be managed if the negative impacts are to be kept to a minimum, and destinations should be aware of such tourists and plan for them accordingly. Demarketing may help over the medium term.

WHERE TO NEXT?
Having examined the process of identifying suitable tourist segments, Chapter 6 moves on to explain the preparation of a tourism development strategy. Building on the previously completed resource audit, the chapter shows how action plans are derived from goals and objectives. Chapter 6 (the tourism development plan) and Chapter 7 (the tourism marketing plan) are complementary and should be read concurrently to help put the broader development strategy into perspective.

FURTHER READING on Selecting Tourists
Kotler, P., Armstrong, G., Saunders, J. and Wang, V. (1999) *Principles of Marketing 2nd European Edition*. New Jersey: Prentice-Hall (in particular Chapters 6, 7 & 9).
Middleton, V.T.C. (1994) *Marketing in travel and tourism* (2nd edition). Oxford: Butterworth-Heinemann.

Segment name	Figures for size of segment	Importance to destination	Benefits sought	Trip characteristics	Personal characteristics
Retired couples	14% of total tourist trips 10% of total tourist spend 1.4 million within 3 hours drive of destination, etc.	Overall 4 Off-peak 1 Importance increasing	Relaxation peace and quiet, sense of tradition and history, physical comfort	2–3 nights arrive by car, book direct, off-peak arrival, £30–£40 ppn spend, rely on word of mouth, joint decision, etc.	Retired married couples age 65+, city-based socio-economic groups ABC1, house or flat owners, etc.

Table 5.9: Destination X portfolio of tourist segments

CHAPTER SIX

How do we get them? Part 1
Preparing a development plan

INTRODUCTION

Tourism development planning takes place at all levels of activity, from the national and international level to local communities and individual attractions. In many respects, the general principles of planning are similar at these different levels (i.e. resource assessment, market analysis, development strategy and marketing plan), however, the practical application or operation of these plans are usually quite different.

At the national level, development planning tends to reflect broad economic objectives, and is mainly indicative of what can be achieved rather than a prescribed set of activities. Much attention is directed at facilitating growth, with greatest emphasis on marketing and technical support to lower levels of operation. At the local or destination level, however, the focus of tourism development planning becomes much more involved. After all, it is here where the impacts of tourism are most acute, where visitors are actually served, resources used and the tourism experience is created.

Tourism development planning at the destination level is primarily about programming change in the use of resources in some prescribed fashion. Resources are analysed, markets assessed, impacts considered, goals established and actions defined. The local tourism development plan provides a framework through which the destination's tourism policy is acted upon (see Chapter 3), ensuring that the development which does occur is appropriate to the area, reflects local values, and is a benefit to the tourism industry itself.

Tourism planning is critical at the destination level if communities are to maintain the integrity of their local resources, while providing the level of visitor satisfaction necessary for tourism to succeed. If destinations cannot offer a positive experience of place, people and activities which satisfy visitor expectations, while protecting their resource base from overuse, the outcome will tend to be less than satisfactory for all concerned.

Given the analysis of resources, markets, impacts and policies in previous chapters, this book now sets out to discuss the basic steps in defining goals and objectives as a core element of the *tourism development plan*. The context and content of the *tourism marketing plan* is then examined in Chapter 7.

THE TOURISM STRATEGY PROCESS

One key function of the *Tourism Resource Audit* (discussed in Chapter 4) was to examine a destination's tourism strengths and weakness from a supply point of view. The outcome of this review should have identified the area's key *assets* (where resource features were considered as 'good'), as well as a number of *issues* or *concerns* needing further attention (resource elements considered 'satisfactory' or in 'need of improvement'). In Chapter 5 the discussion focused on identifying key groups of visitors (or target markets) most likely to use these local resources and provide the greatest benefit to the destination. The task now is to bring these two functions together in the preparation of the tourism development plan.

Similar to the steps of the *tourism resource audit*, the process of preparing a *tourism development plan* is a multi-stage activity, which seeks to:

♦ identify development opportunities and constraints (based on the evaluation of supply and demand previously completed);

♦ set goals and objectives for development which address those issues needing attention in the short, medium and longer term;

♦ define a series of action steps designed to achieve these goals and objectives within some specified time frame.

STAGE 1 – Identifying Opportunities & Constraints

By completing the resource audit steps discussed in Chapter 4, a number of issues or concerns with tourism will probably have been identified as needing some form of attention, or in need of improvement. However, as this initial analysis was fairly broad (i.e. including all resource features) it will usually be necessary at this stage to break these points down further into a more manageable set of issues and opportunities. In addition, as not all issues will be of equal concern or importance (with some needing a more immediate response than others), these will need to be ranked in some order of priority.

The task of simplifying and ranking the initial review into a workable set of issues involves a four-step process:

Step 1: Using the 'overall assessment' column on the initial audit form (Appendix 4j, page 88) transfer all resource elements listed as in 'need of improvement' to the *Tourism Issues Table* (Figure 6.1, page 111). These resource elements will tend to be those aspects of the destination which cause the greatest level of concern for tourism, and would generally take priority in the tourism development plan.

In so doing, the Tourism Issues Table should also include a brief summary of the key points which determined that initial overall rating (i.e. its *quality*, *uniqueness* and/or *appeal*). This step is designed not only to help destinations begin to identify potential changes or improvements to the resource, but also to highlight anything which may stand in the way of future development action. For example:

> a large river-front setting may at first seem a significant tourism opportunity, but closer inspection shows little visitor activity. In terms of *'quality'*, limited access points are seen to restrict visitor use. However, this section of the river is *unique* because of a small island situated in the middle of the channel. This island happens to be a nesting site for local wildfowl, which includes a rare and interesting species. Given the uniqueness but limited access, this feature was seen as *needing improvement* on the Resource Audit, if it was to play a more central role in the destination's tourism profile.

If nothing was considered to be in need of improvement, then the initial analysis was probably not rigorous enough. It is unlikely that everything is ever perfect in terms of tourism supply and demand.

When auditing resource elements for tourism it is important to remember that while some features may be considered adequate or good in the present (and thus not a current concern), what happens in the future may change this point of view. Continual monitoring of activity remains a vital element of any development strategy (see Chapter 9).

Step 2: The next step is to identify which groups of existing visitors, or expected tourist markets are most relevant to that particular resource feature or element. An understanding of the markets to which different resources will appeal is fundamental in preparing a tourism development strategy. For example:

> the river setting and wildfowl population will not appeal to all
> visitor markets. However, some of the destinations key visitor
> markets would find this 'attraction' of interest. Further
> development of this resource would thus seem worthwhile, not only
> for its appeal to the destination's key visitor markets and
> contribution to the industry, but because local environmental
> improvements are a benefit to the local community as well.

Current and potential visitor markets should always play a central role when considering development opportunities. The analysis of visitors discussed in Chapter 5 should provide a good understanding of local tourism markets and the destination's tourism market profiles. Having this type of information is important so that resource improvements are directed at those areas which will most likely affect the destination's more important target markets. In other words, resource improvements are directed at those visitors who are most likely to appreciate the improvement, and in turn represent the greatest benefit to the destination.

Step 3: Once the key resource issues or concerns have been recorded, and market(s) listed, the next step is to identify the potential *opportunities* for tourism use of that resource, and any *constraints* facing its further development. For example:

> in terms of 'opportunities', a riverside trail or walkway could be
> improved; viewing and seating points established; interpretation
> panels installed, explaining the significance of the island; river
> tours/ ferry services, park development or improvement, fishing or
> marina developments, and commercial links could also be
> established which highlight the local 'wildfowl' experience.

However, while some aspects of the local resource base may seem central to the tourism product and in need of improvement, there may be constraints on what can actually be done. For example:

> in terms of 'constraints', these could include competing land-use
> claims for the riverside which take priority over tourism use; owner-
> ship of the riverside area could restrict development opportunities;
> development and interpretation costs could be prohibitive;
> conservation issues may limit use; or a lack of market awareness
> could mean little interest in the outcome of the development.

The purpose of identifying or outlining these opportunities and constraints is to highlight those areas where tourism development effort will make the most significant initial impacts. It should give some indication of where development efforts will most likely be rewarded, and identify where potential problems will emerge. It should also help the destination recognize its limitations in terms of tourism and identify what can or cannot realistically be achieved.

Step 4: The final step at this point in the development process is to rank order the list of problems or concerns. The purpose of ranking is to identify those points which will take priority in preparing the destination's tourism development goals and objectives. Tourism problems or concerns should be ranked on the basis of their importance and link to the destination's key tourism markets, as well as the more viable in terms of taking any action:

♦ higher ranking should accord with issues most directly affecting key target markets, and/or have the most significant impact on the widest groups of visitors;

♦ higher ranking should also accord with those issues or concerns more easily addressed and which will readily show the benefit of action.

Those points ranked the highest will then get the attention they deserve when it comes to writing the action plan. For example:

> as the riverside area represents a key component of the destination's natural tourism resource, it is a major concern. While there may be other features of the destination which should and could be improved, this issue is ranked high on the list of priorities because it relates to key visitor markets and is a high-profile/highly visible element of the destination.

There is little use in giving something a high priority if it will have minimal impact on key visitor markets or will require substantial effort to implement, as these will give limited return on investment and effort in the short term. This is not to suggest that the more difficult problems should be ignored, but rather it is important to address concerns which can and will lead to visible and positive results in the short term, which helps add further support to continued and future effort and activity in the longer term.

At this point in the planning process, having completed all the previous steps, the destination should have:

Resource feature	Resource feature Issues (quality, uniqueness, appeal)	Key Markets Served	Tourism Development Opportunities	Tourism Development Constraints	Rank*
Natural:					
Cultural:					
Events:					
Activities:					
Services:					

*Rank Resource Features according to level of priority in terms of action.

Figure 6.1: Tourism Issues Table

♦ a concise, ranked listing of development issues;

♦ a good understanding of its tourist profile;

♦ some idea of what needs to be done to improve tourism potential.

The reason for assessing development opportunities and constraints is to provide direction and a focus for future development. The destination should now be ready to begin thinking more about the next stage of the tourism development process: *setting development goals and objectives.*

STAGE 2 – Setting Development Goals and Objectives
Stage 1 of the strategy process (discussed above) is designed to help destinations evaluate their past and present conditions of tourism supply and demand, providing an answer to the question: 'where are we now?' Stage 2 looks to the future, and asks: 'where do we want to be?', or 'what would we like to accomplish through the development of tourism?' The tourism development strategy provides the link between the *status quo* and 'where we'd like to be'.

Setting goals and objectives forms a core element of any strategic planning process. It creates a bridge between development policy and the series of actions designed to pursue that policy. A destination's tourism policy is effectively a broad mission statement (see Chapter 3) which steers development activity in a particular direction. Goals and objectives represent the framework through which this policy is defined and acted upon.

The system of setting goals and objectives represents a means to the end of putting that policy into practice. Without a clear set of specified goals and objectives, a destination will have nothing to guide its activities, assess whether it has been successful, or be able to show what progress has actually been made (see Figure 6.2, page 113).

Tourism Goals provide a general direction or focus for the tourism policy. They are:

♦ statements of intent or desire about the way tourism should be developed to improve its potential and mitigate problems;

♦ continuous – they are never actually reached, but always pursued;

♦ short, clear and concise statements outlining the direction of future development;

♦ the foundations for setting more precise objectives which follow.

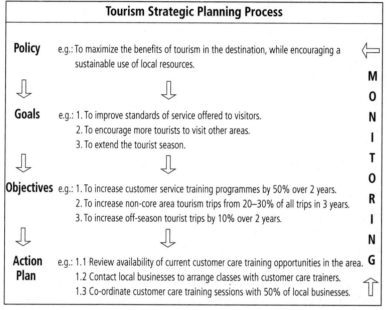

Figure 6.2: Tourism Strategic Planning Process

<u>**Tourism Objectives**</u> are more specific than goals. Each goal may have several objectives. Objectives are meant to accomplish tourism goals and address tourism issues identified in the resource analysis. They break goals down into detailed statements of intent and define how the goals will be realized. They provide a definite direction for tourism and act as a benchmark for measuring success in the future. As such, tourism development objectives must be:

♦ quantifiable or measurable;

♦ achievable within a specific time period;

♦ concise, specific and clear to anyone reading them;

♦ realistic, not some impractical wish list.

Tourism Action Steps then provide the 'who, what, where and how', the detail of how these goals and objectives will be pursued. Tourism actions state what precisely will be done, when it will be done and by whom. It is very likely that several action steps will be linked with each objective. Tourism Action Steps are therefore:

♦ specific as to what exactly should be done, and by whom;

♦ are precise so as to avoid ambiguity of purpose;

♦ have a specific time-scale and expected outcome;

♦ can be delegated to individuals or groups to undertake.

Writing Tourism Goals

Writing goals and objectives can be a quite difficult if not frustrating task. But it is a necessary element of the tourism development process, to ensure development action and activities are complementary to each other and all pulling in the same direction.

Tourism goals tend to arise in one of two ways, generally depending on the level of planning being considered. At the national level, goals are often developed via further elaboration of national policy. At the destination, however, while goals are meant to reflect local policy, they tend to come from the strategic planning process and address issues identified during the resource audit, market analysis and the *Tourism Issues Table* discussed earlier.

Tourism goals should be relatively simple statements, concerned with such fundamental things as improving standards of service offered to tourists, increasing the diversity of local attractions, or encouraging tourists to visit a wider area in the destination (i.e. spreading the load).

Those issues and opportunities that are ranked the highest in the *Tourism Issues Table* should become the key elements in determining initial development goals. By addressing each of the major areas of concern highlighted in the initial analysis, most problem points will be reconsidered in the setting of goals and objectives. For example:

♦ **Issue 1**: During the analysis phase it was discovered that there were problems with the diversity of attractions in the destination. Tourists had complained that there weren't enough

contd

things to see and/or do in the area, especially if they were to stay more than just a few hours. In this case the goal might be:

♦ **Goal 1**: 'to increase the volume and diversity of tourism opportunities in the destination'.

♦ **Issue 2**: Another problem area was seen to exist with the services available at the tourist information centre; some businesses were not tourist friendly; and the destination suffered from a lack of identity. These issues of customer service and hospitality might suggest that the destination would need to focus part of its development efforts on seeking to improve its hospitality services. In this case the goal might simply be:

♦ **Goal 2**: 'to improve the quality of tourism hospitality in the destination'.

♦ **Issue 3**: The market analysis also highlighted another key weakness for the destination. Most current visitors fell into only one or two key market groups. Any future change in travel patterns, preference or other aspect of market competition could lead to a significant decline in overall visitor numbers. In this case, another goal might be:

♦ **Goal 3**: 'to increase the diversity of tourist markets coming to the destination'.

As these examples suggest, tourism goals are meant to be continuous. The objectives and action steps which follow will work towards a particular goal, but will never fully achieve it. This is because there is always room for improvement, with the whole tourism planning process being one of on-going evaluation and review. As conditions change, priorities shift, and issues become resolved, a new set of goals and priorities need to be considered.

Once the initial tourism goals have been set, the next step is to develop a series of objectives, each designed to respond to one of these goals.

Writing Tourism Objectives

Writing tourism objectives is a five-step process using the *Goals and Objectives Table* (see Figure 6.3). Like tourism goals, objectives flow from the strategic planning process. They are broadly conceived to address tourism issues and opportunities as expressed by goals, but precise enough to be readily obtainable within a given time frame.

Tourism Development Goals and Objectives			
Goal:			
Key issue or opportinuty:			
Objectives:	Markets affected	Time-scale	Rank

Figure 6.3: Tourism Development Goals and Objectives

Setting tourism objectives, however, can be a little more difficult than deciding on development goals. Yet this need not always be the case. By focusing on one goal and issue at a time, the process becomes much simpler. Each goal may have several objectives, and objectives can relate to more than one goal. However, for the sake of simplicity, each objective should initially be written in relation to only one goal at a time. If an objective will help achieve more than one goal, so be it, however, problems tend to emerge when trying to write objectives which cover too many issues all at once. They become vague, difficult to implement and imposs-ible to measure.

Step 1: Restate each goal, one at a time, each on a separate table. Summarize the key issue or opportunity which that broad goal is meant to address. Each table should relate to one goal and one of the key issues identified in the previous stage of the analysis. For example:

> If one of the top-ranked issues previously identified was a lack of quality information for visitors to take away, such as local maps and brochures, etc., then a goal to which this issue relates might be:
>
> ♦ **to improve the quality of tourism hospitality.**

As the initial set of goals have been written in relation to the top-ranking issues, the series of objectives which follow should then reflect the destination's top priorities in terms of tourism improvements.

Step 2: Briefly re-examine the issues that are associated with this particular goal. There are likely to be a number of sub-issues which can be considered and addressed through a series of specific and related objectives. For example:

> If a key issue was considered to be '*a lack of quality information for visitors to take away, such as local maps and brochures, etc.*', the sub-issues might be:
>
> (a) the lack of a quality destination map for visitors showing key locations of attractions and services;
>
> (b) the lack of quality brochures which serve to inform and promote the destination's different attractions.

Writing objectives which deal with these issues (and which work towards the original goal), becomes one of restating these issues or problems in a positive light. For example:

> ♦ **Sub-issue A**: '*the lack of a quality destination map for visitors showing key locations of attractions and services*'.
>
> can be reworded as an objective,
>
> ♦ **Objective A**: '*to provide a new map of the destination highlighting the location of local attractions and visitor services*'.

unrealized ambition, which can easily destroy motivation and all the hard work that has already gone into the planning process.

Step 4: The next step therefore is to conduct a *reality check* and re-evaluate the objectives. It may be necessary to rethink an objective, downgrade what it seeks to achieve, or break it down into smaller objectives with a more realistic time frame. For example:

♦ **Objective B**: *'to encourage all local attractions each to supply one new brochure ...'* may be too ambitious within a six-month time-scale.

It also may be that the destination needs first to produce a general guidance note on what basic or minimum tourist information the local tourism committee would like to see in these brochures.

As a result it may be that this objective should be given a longer time frame, or rewritten with an emphasis on encouraging the destination's *key attractions* first to produce the brochures, rather than all attractions, at least during this first phase of development activity.

It is very likely that during the previous four steps, several different objectives will have been developed. However, not all of these can be accomplished at the same time, nor will they all have an equal impact on the various tourism issues they are meant to address. It is therefore important to give some *priority* to these objectives in terms of what will be tackled first, and so on.

Step 5: The final step in setting goals and objectives (before moving on to prepare tourism action steps in STAGE 3), is to assess all the objectives together and then to establish some order of relative priority or importance.

To rank the objectives in order of importance, all goals and objectives are listed on one table (see Figure 6.4). Each member of the committee preparing the development strategy should then have their own identical copy of this table (or some form of list which relates to the 'master table'), and individually rank each objective out of 20 (irrespective of the goal to which it relates). The higher the number, the higher the priority or importance of that particular objective. While there may be many objectives to choose from, ranking should be limited to what individuals feel are the seven to ten most important objectives. By using a scale of 1 to 20 it allows for a greater flexibility and emphasis to be placed on different objectives.

These 'top priority' objectives should be chosen on the basis of:

♦ how well they enhance or help improve the local tourism industry;

♦ their relationship with the destination's key tourism markets;

♦ those which can realistically be achieved with local resources and effort;

♦ how quickly they can be achieved;

♦ their visibility to the wider public.

Goal	Objective Priority List	Rank
	Objectives	

Figure 6.4: Objective Priority List

When complete, the overall importance or rank of an objective is then determined simply by the sum of individual rankings for each objective. The objective with the highest total score becomes the top priority, the second-highest score becomes the number 2 objective and so on. In the event of a tie, a simple majority vote should be taken in order to reach a quick decision.

This initial priority list sets out the destination's most immediate concerns and provides a sense of direction for the subsequent *Action Plan*. By limiting the list of priority objectives to 7 to 10, the destination will be in a better position to make an immediate impact on tourism and realize its own accomplishment. Achieving these will help build confidence, support and pride, allowing subsequent objectives to be addressed. Once the initial set of objectives have been dealt with, the process can be repeated and those remaining objectives can be reassessed with a new order of priority.

Writing out goals and objectives in this fashion may seem a tedious and somewhat laborious exercise, but it is essential to get these points down on paper. Writing things down works very well to help focus the mind and promote action. Once opportunities and constraints, issues, goals and objectives have been written out they can be altered, amended, edited, ignored, added to, improved or deleted as the case may be. However, experience has shown that when this stage is skipped over the development actions pursued, in response to key problems often fail actually to address the original issue or concern.

When the process of writing our goals and objectives is complete, the emphasis then shifts to devising a set of actions which translate these goals and objectives into practical activity – the action plan.

STAGE 3 – Devising the Action Plan

In its crudest form, the tourism development strategy is essentially a series of action steps designed to help realize or put into practice some predetermined tourism policy. Devising a set of actions is the last stage of the basic development plan, setting out the destination's tourism objectives, describing in detail how this will be achieved, who will do it and when the expected outcome will be realized. Tourism action steps are designed to provide the means and method of reaching a particular tourism objective. More often than not, each objective will require several steps to reach a conclusion.

The tourism action plan is effectively a detailed sequence of steps, describing exactly what is to be done and in what order of activity. The action steps are very specific and if written properly, leave no room for ambiguity as to what is expected. However, actions steps are only an estimate of what needs to be done to achieve each objective. They are not absolute, and it may be that as work proceeds subsequent actions may need amending to complete the task as new issues arise or problems are encountered.

Goal:

Objective: **Rank no.**

Issue or opportunity:

Action steps	By whom	Time frame start	finish	Outcome
1				
2				
3				
4				
5				
6				

Figure 6.5: Tourism Actions Table

Writing Tourism Action Steps

Tourism Actions Steps are prepared by taking one objective at a time, starting with the top-ranked objective from the *Objective Priority List* (Figure 6.4). Using the *Tourism Actions Table* (see Figure 6.5), restate the key issue, goal and objective which the actions are meant to address before beginning to write the individual actions steps. This information will help in establishing and identifying the background to the actions steps which follow.

Step 1: Start to write out actions steps by briefly stating what needs to be done, in a step-by-step fashion, to meet the objective. For example:

---

if the objective is:

♦ *'to provide a new pocket map of the destination, highlighting the location of local attractions and visitor services'*

the actions steps might be:

1. Obtain detailed costs estimates of producing the new town map, including printing costs and cartographic fees.

2. Contact local tourist businesses, chamber of commerce and town council to seek support, sponsorship and funding for the map.

3. Identify the location of all attractions and tourist services on a basic street map of the destination.

4. Decide and locate which other features will also be included on the map.

5. Find a cartographer or graphic artist, preferably local, who can prepare a stylized map of the destination including these key features, attractions and tourist services.

6. Find a printer, preferably local, who can print the quality and quantity of maps required.

Step 2: When each action has been identified the next step is to assign someone with the responsibility to complete the task. This should also include some indication of the expected start and completion of the task(s). Action steps should be listed in chronological order, with one step normally commenced before the next is considered. When the action steps are actually undertaken and complete, a note on the result of the action should be entered on the *Tourism Actions Table* as a record of the activity.

If it is difficult to identify any action steps for any particular objective it may be the objective is too vague, overambitious, or even unrealistic in what it seeks to achieve. If this is the case, it will be necessary to rework the objective to reflect more specific outcomes, break it down into smaller more manageable sub-objectives, or even delete it altogether. Similarly, if it is unclear what is actually required by the action steps or if there is some ambiguity as to how this will be achieved, then those action steps will also need to be restated and be more specific.

WHAT TO DO NEXT?

Once the complete set of actions steps have been prepared for the 7–10 priority objectives previously identified, then all that remains at this point, is to begin to put these plans into practice and begin to implement the actions. This of course is not the end of the tourism development strategy, and the belief that once attractions are in place visitors will flood in, is a common mistake in tourism development. Rarely will destinations sell themselves.

If these actions are intended to attract more visitors, encourage them to stay longer, create more of an economic benefit, and perhaps encourage them to come back again in the future, then a *marketing plan* will be necessary. Marketing, however, is so much more than simply selling the destination at one point in time. As much as it is important to understand the opportunities and constraints, assets and liabilities of tourism supply, it is equally important to understand the needs, wants and wishes of the tourists themselves (tourism demand).

The marketing plan, like the development plan discussed above, needs to be thought through, organized, realistic and written down. The discussion in Chapter 5 focused on better understanding a destination's tourism markets (the who, what, where, etc.), now the point is to link this information with the actions developed in this chapter and prepare a tourism marketing plan. To this end, the next chapter outlines the basic structure and steps involved in preparing a marketing plan for tourism destinations.

FURTHER READING *for Developing a Tourism Plan*

Blank, Uel (1989) *The Community Tourism Industry Imperative: the necessity, the opportunities, its potential*. State College, PA: Venture.
Gunn, C. (1994) *Tourism Planning: basics, concepts, cases* (3rd edition). London: Taylor & Francis Ltd.
Mill, R.C. and Morrison, A.M. (1985) *The Tourism System: an introductory text*. London: Prentice-Hall International.

CHAPTER SEVEN

How do we get them? Part 2
Developing the marketing plan

INTRODUCTION

Too often, marketing is seen by destinations as synonymous with promotion or communications activity. In fact, marketing is a strategic process that aims to fit the resources of a destination to the opportunities existing in the market. It is as much about retaining the tourist as it is about winning new business. Additionally, it is complementary to planning, as will become apparent in this chapter. Indeed, the glamour often associated with marketing is in reality based on much hard work behind the scenes. The glamour without the preceding analysis and strategic framework often results in a series of inconsistent communication campaigns that confuse the tourist and do nothing to develop a solid proposition. So, although this chapter focuses on the communications mix as a unique contribution from marketing practice, it is rooted in a wider appreciation of the hard graft.

A marketing plan is a written, working document that should be prepared by a cross-section of the destination community (see Chapter 3), ideally under the guidance of a marketing practitioner, or by an independent marketing consultant working in close collaboration with the destination (see Chapter 10). Its content, as copies or verbal presentations, must be freely disseminated amongst those with an interest in the area's tourism. The plan needs to be strong enough to give direction and unity of purpose, yet flexible enough to allow businesses to pursue their own initiatives. Unlike a marketing plan for a commercial organization, the destination marketing plan relies on co-operation and persuasion. It is imperative that those working with the plan feel a sense of ownership.

Essentially, there are two different time-scales attached to marketing plans and the nature of these plans will vary accordingly:

- **the 3–5 year strategic marketing plan** sets the direction for the annual plans and the broad outline for activities.

- **the annual or tactical marketing plan** sets the detailed actions and methods of monitoring achievement. The sum of the annual plans should meet the objectives set in the strategic marketing plan for the relevant time period.

Strategic marketing plan (3–5 years)		Annual or tactical marketing plan (1 year)	
Situation analysis	external internal	Summary of	situation analysis SWOT
Forecast		Key tourist/other segments	
Key factors for success		Annual marketing objectives	
Distinctive competencies		Product	objectives strategies tactics
SWOT analysis		Price	objectives strategies tactics
Key tourist/other segments		Distribution	objectives strategies tactics
Positioning statement		Communication	objectives strategies tactics
Marketing objectives		Monitoring, evaluation and control	
Strategies for	product price distribution communication		
Evaluation & control			

Table 7.1: Comparison of Strategic and Annual Marketing Plans

Take the analogy of planning a car trip from points A to B. First, you would investigate the alternative route options and then outline the pre-ferred choice and approximate timings and cost (strategic marketing plan). Secondly, you would work on a detailed plan; time of day to leave, what to pack, car maintenance, *en route* stops, who is driving and so on (tactical marketing plan). It would be pointless to plan the detail before some thought was given to where you wanted to go and the best route of getting there. The same can be said for marketing plans. Table 7.1 contrasts the typical headings in a strategic marketing plan with the typical headings in an annual tactical marketing plan. An understanding of the content of the different headings will develop with this chapter.

The marketing process and the resultant marketing plan focus on answering four classic questions:

♦ **where are we now?** [situation analysis and SWOT];

♦ **where do we want to be?** [marketing objectives];

♦ **how do we get there?** [strategies and tactics];

♦ **how do we know if we've got there?** [monitoring, evaluation and control].

This chapter will address each of these questions in turn, indicating other relevant chapters as appropriate.

WHERE ARE WE KNOW?

Before a destination can plan for the future, it is essential that it has an objective grasp of its current situation and of the trends affecting it. The situation analysis (or its fuller version, the marketing audit) encompasses both external and internal factors. Information can be obtained from a combination of secondary and primary research (see Chapter 9), depending on availability and resource constraints (here Chapter 4 is particularly relevant). Not information for information's sake, but as a sound basis for action.

Situation Analysis at the Macro Level

At the macro level, the analysis focuses on the wider environment in which the destination operates. It investigates facts and trends that are external to the destination as a product but relevant for decision-making. These external factors in the environment can be categorized as:

♦ *political and legal factors*, such as political stability, nature of political organization and concentration of power, statutory planning requirements, consumer protection legislation, visa and entry requirements, green legislation, accommodation classification and grading, health and safety legislation, national and local government support for tourism, international relations and so on.

♦ **economic factors**, such as stage in business cycle, distribution of wealth, balance of payments, inflation/deflation rates, banking system, interest rates, saving and expenditure patterns, taxation, discretionary incomes, balance between private and public sector ownership, employment patterns in terms of occupation, skills, costs, availability, part-time/job share structure, seasonality, gender etc., foreign exchange rates, issues around emerging currencies, etc.

♦ **social, demographic and cultural factors**, such as government social policy, e.g. social tourism, cultural norms and values, language, religion, social roles, gender issues, racial issues, standard of living, life expectancy and healthy life expectancy, balance between work and leisure participation, travel habits, migration patterns, class structure and mobility, attitudes towards environment and consumption, distribution of population spatially, degree of urbanization, educational levels, age/gender profiles, household size and structure, marriage and divorce rates, levels and types of crime and so on.

♦ **technological factors**, such as knowledge base and availability, Internet usage, development of destination databases, alternative sources of power, advances in transport technology, speeds of adoption, video conferences, computerized global distribution systems and so on.

Information on the macro environment should be collected on a continuous basis – it is a matter of sketching the patterns and scanning for signs of change. The headings for the standard analysis of the external macro environment form an English acronym, PEST. Hence, this type of analysis is sometimes referred to as a PEST analysis. A summary of the key points is often presented on a single page of the marketing plan.

Situation Analysis at the Micro Level

At the micro level of the situation analysis, the destination examines those factors influencing its immediate business environment. At the micro level, the external factors in the environment can be categorized as:

♦ ***markets/tourists***, in terms of who is visiting the destination, their profile, what tourism components are they buying or using, where are they buying or deciding (in home country, at home, through travel agent, *en route*, at local TIC, etc.), when are they buying or arriving (seasonality), how do they buy or decide (on impulse, after consulting with the family, after an extensive search for information, using which criteria, etc.), and why are they buying or which benefits are they looking for. The who, what, where, when, how and why are six fundamental questions asked about markets in the situation analysis.

♦ ***suppliers***, in terms of who contributes to the destination product, outside of the actual producers of the tourism components. This might include market research agencies, advertising agencies, print companies, trainers and educational establishments, independent consultants, and so on. Are they locally based? What are their numbers, skills, strengths and weaknesses?

♦ ***distributors***, in terms of who helps to sell the destination to the tourist. This might include the TIC network outside of the immediate area, the national tourist board or government agency, incoming tour operators, coach/ferry/cruise operators, wholesalers, overseas tour operators, specific interest groups such as clubs and societies, and travel agencies. What are the structural trends? Again, what are their numbers, skills, strengths and weaknesses?

♦ ***competitors***, especially direct competition. Which destinations offer a comparable product to your own that might act as a substitute in the marketplace? What are their strengths and weaknesses compared to yours? Distance from major tourist-generating areas is one important factor, but it is not the only one of relevance. How successfully are the competition positioned in the marketplace? What are their plans, resources and skills? Indirect competitors or organizations which offer products that compete for the discretionary income and leisure time of potential tourists, might also be listed. Wider in scope, such competition may come in the form of urban health clubs, television and video manufacturers, home-improvement superstores, garden and plant centres, and so forth.

Tourism destinations should try to assess any options for alliances. Other destinations may offer a complementary product, creating opportunities for expanding the total market by developing twin centre holidays, unifying themed trails or scenic routes, combination attraction ticket schemes, and other ideas. A neighbouring destination is not automatically a direct competitor. There may be possibilities for co-operation from which both areas would benefit.

As with the PEST analysis, the key points from the investigation of the micro environment are often summarized on one page of the marketing plan.

Internal Situation Analysis

The internal situation analysis is a self-analysis. It critically reviews the destination. Chapter 4 is very relevant, and this section will not replicate material already covered. The term self-analysis should be treated cautiously; the internal audit may be better done by an independent consultant able to evaluate the situation dispassionately. Objectivity is the key. A review of the marketing resources can be broken down as:

♦ *marketing objectives and strategies*, an evaluation of past performance and an assessment of the reasons behind any shortfall;

♦ *marketing organization*, an evaluation of current structures and their effectiveness;

♦ *marketing systems*, an evaluation of the marketing research and information process, the marketing planning process and the methods by which marketing activity is monitored and controlled;

♦ *marketing functions*, an evaluation of the current product, prices, communications and distribution used by the destination. These four functions are commonly referred to as the basic marketing mix. For example, for distribution, how much business does the destination achieve through each distribution channel, and what is the ratio of sales to the cost of servicing this channel? Which channels are best for last-minute business or for precious out-of-season business?

These findings should be contrasted with any close competitors, creating a relative verdict for marketing resources. As with the external assessments of the situation, the internal audit is usually summarized on one page of the marketing plan.

Developing on from the Situation Analysis

Having summarized the three parts of the situation analysis by highlighting the key points, the destination should then consider:

♦ *a forecast of these key points*, showing how they might develop in the future. Outlines of future scenarios can be invaluable when mapping out a vision for the destination or for comparing alternative strategies. Forecasts also help prepare any assumptions considered necessary to set the context for objectives;

♦ *key factors for success (KFS)*, or factors that each destination competing for similar business must get right if it is going to be successful in the medium to long term. It is hard to imagine a scheduled airline even surviving without a good central reservation system. Customer care may prove a KFS for destinations (see Chapter 8). Others may include developing a unique identity rooted in the local area, or grappling with environmental issues. A destination should compare its performance on KFS against that of competitors;

♦ *distinctive competencies*, or skills and advantages that a destination possesses that could be developed to give long-term advantage over competitors. The best distinctive competencies are those that are unique to the destination and tricky for competitors to emulate. Ideally, a cluster of competencies should be identified.

SWOT Analysis

The SWOT analysis is the culmination of the detailed work involved in answering the question 'where are we now?' Often presented as a single-page summary in matrix form (see Figure 7.1), the SWOT analysis is an honest and sometimes painful portrayal of the destination's strengths and weaknesses relative to the competition, and of the opportunities and threats that it faces. For this reason, commercial companies are wary of releasing such documents in case they are perused by competitors. The SWOT analysis examines the destination's:

♦ *strengths*, relative to the competition, derived from the internal analysis. Strengths may be ranked or scored to indicate importance.

♦ ***weaknesses***, relative to the competition, derived from the internal analysis. Weaknesses may be ranked or scored to indicate importance.

♦ ***opportunities***, taken from the external situation analysis, can be assessed in terms of time-scale (immediate, medium, long term), importance in terms of benefit to the destination and likelihood of success.

♦ ***threats***, taken from the external situation analysis, can be assessed in terms of their time-scale, importance in terms of severity of negative impact on the destination and probability of occurrence.

For the purposes of the destination's marketing plan, the headings given in Table 7.1 relating to the question 'where are we now?' are fleshed out more thoroughly in the strategic marketing plan. The tactical marketing plan presents the vital points in summarized form; the practitioner can always refer back to the strategic plan for elaboration.

Strengths	Weaknesses
•	•
•	•
•	•
•	•
•	•
•	•
Opportunities	Threats
•	•
•	•
•	•
•	•
•	•
•	•

Figure 7.1: Framework for a SWOT Analysis
Importance rating 1–5
Probability of success/occurrence 1–5
Time-scale I, M, L

WHERE DO WE WANT TO BE?

Objectives express in concrete form the vision of where the destination would like to be after a given lapse of time, say three or five years. Marketing objectives focus chiefly on markets and products. Table 7.2

illustrates a sample of possible marketing objectives. In practice, objectives are individual to the destination – of course, for they flow from the work put into the SWOT analysis. Table 7.2 raises a number of points about marketing objectives for destinations:

- ◆ annual objectives arise from the longer-term strategic objectives. There is a logical consistency from time-scale to time-scale, creating a cascade of higher- and lower-order objectives.

- ◆ objectives are compatible with each other. There is internal consistency. In the examples given for destination x, the objectives for visit numbers, length of stay, expenditure and seasonality can be cross-compared and seen to be pulling in the same direction. For example, the increase in expenditure also represents an average spend increase per visit from £12.50 in 2000 (20,000 visitors) to £16.67 in 2003 (30,000 visitors). So, they are relevant to one another.

- ◆ objectives are a mix of readily quantifiable and essentially qualitative aims. Figures and percentages or ratios can be attached to hard objectives, allowing for easier measurement. Soft objectives that tackle quality, positioning or customer care, can still be measured through marketing research. All objectives should be measurable.

- ◆ stated objectives must be as specific as possible. For example, it is more specific to state a time-scale as running from January 1998 to January 2001 than simply to say 'over the next three years'.

- ◆ objectives need to be timed as, without this, success in achieving objectives cannot be measured. Breaking down tactical objectives into monthly or weekly targets allows contingency plans to be used to close any gaps before achieving the objective becomes a matter of crisis management. Without a deadline, there can be no control mechanism.

- ◆ objectives should be achievable. A benefit of good objectives is that they stretch and motivate participants, but overambitious statements lose both credibility and participant enthusiasm.

Strategic marketing objectives	Tactical marketing objectives (1 year)
• numbers of tourist visits to destination expressed in actual figures ('000s) and/or as a % increase/decrease on current figures. Time-scale? e.g. to increase the number of tourist visits to destination x from 20,000 to 30,000, a 50% increase from 1999 to 2002	• numbers of tourist visits broken down to annual target in line with 10,000 increase (e.g. 6,000). By international/domestic visits? By key segments? Key nationalities? New versus repeat business?
• expenditure by tourists visiting destination, expressed in actual figures ('000s etc.) and/or as a % increase on current figures. Time-scale? e.g. to increase expenditure by tourists visiting destination x from (£)250,000 to (£)500,000, a 100% increase from 1999 to 2002	• expenditure figures broken down to annual target in line with (£)250,000 increase (e.g. £90,000). By spend per head? Spend per visit? By key segment? By destination component (accommodation, attractions, etc.)?
• length of stay of tourists visiting the destination, expressed in actual figures (days/nights) and/or as % increase on current figures. Time-scale? e.g. to increase the average length of stay of tourists visiting destination x from 1 night to 3 nights from 1999 to 2002	• length of stay broken down by key segments? By accommodation components (hotels, self-catering, private pensions, etc.)? By month/season?
• extend the season for tourist visits to the destination, expressed in actual figures and as % increase on current business in shoulder and trough months, e.g. to extend the season for destination x in shoulder and trough months from 5,000 visits to 10,000, a 100% increase from 1999 to 2002. * applies to expenditure/length of stay * applies to spatial dispersion/concentration of tourists visits/expenditure	• extend the season for destination x in shoulder and trough months broken down to annual target in line with 5,000 increase (e.g. 2,000). By key segment? By shoulder or trough month? By destination component?
• strengthen positioning or reposition the destination in the minds of key segments, e.g. to strengthen the current positioning of destination x as a historic market town offering value for money	• year-on-year improvement shown by measurement? By key segments? (Use of surveys and/or focus groups)
• improve standards of service and consistency of delivery throughout the destination, e.g. to improve the standards of service and consistency of delivery at destination x	• year-on-year improvement shown by measurement of satisfaction levels? By destination component? By key segments? (Use of surveys and/or focus groups)
• increase numbers/skills/participation of tourism suppliers at the destination, e.g. to increase the number of tourism suppliers participating in group marketing activities from 15 to 30, a 100% increase from 1999 to 2002	• by tourism component? By type of skill?

Table 7.2: Illustrative Marketing Objectives for Destination X

Commercial organizations also set out marketing objectives relating to market share and profit levels. These are open to a local destination for consideration, but such issues may be more relevant to individual business-es. For a local destination, market share data may be difficult to determine.

Key Tourist Segments

A summary of the profiles of the key tourist segments that:

♦ the destination is most suited to satisfying *vis-à-vis* tourist needs and benefits sought and the strength of the competition (market perspective);

♦ are most able to assist the destination in achieving its objectives (destination perspective).

A destination should work with a portfolio of segments to offer flexibility and opportunities for the individual businesses to address. Chapter 5 investigated the identification and preparation of major groups of tourists in greater detail. Marketing mix decisions are made around the know-ledge of key segments.

Positioning

Positioning is the image of the destination against other destinations that a tourist holds in their mind. Any discrepancy between actual positioning and desired positioning by key segment must be assessed. Indeed, strengthening the positioning or repositioning a destination is a commonly stated market-ing objective. Destinations should realize that improvements to the product may be necessary before any attempt is made to correct the positioning. Perceptual maps can be used to represent positioning statements pictorially or graphically where research data is collected (see Figure 7.2, page 136).

HOW DO WE GET THERE?

Strategies are the routes used to achieve objectives, and, as different routes are available, the destination needs to make choices. For the strategic mar-keting plan, a destination might consider the following choices:

♦ sell more of the existing product to repeat tourists (increased frequency) or to sell the existing product to new tourists from existing tourist segments (segment penetration);

♦ sell the existing product to new tourist segments (segment development);

♦ sell a new product to existing tourist segments (product development);

♦ sell a new product to new tourist segments (diversification).

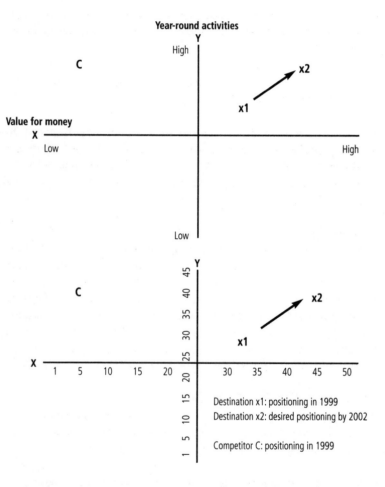

Destination x1: positioning in 1999
Destination x2: desired positioning by 2002

Competitor C: positioning in 1999

Figure 7.2: Perceptual Maps to Support Positioning Statements

The level of risk involved and the required investment increases from frequency through to diversification. This framework (a simplified Ansoff matrix) is related directly to destination objectives in the strategic gap analysis shown in Figure 7.3. It suggests that a destination should first assess the potential of increased frequency to close the gap between the line of inaction and set objectives as the lowest-risk option, and then move logically through the levels of risk until the strategic gap is finally closed.

For the strategic marketing plan, strategies need to be decided for each element of the marketing mix, or those factors controlled by the destination marketing team. These basic marketing mix elements can be categorized as product, price, distribution, and communications. In practice, these categories are not mutually exclusive. All four need to be co-ordinated so that they support each other in meeting objectives, and the strategies are a summary or overview of the proposed activities.

For the tactical marketing plan, the strategies of the longer time-scale are converted into marketing mix objectives at the annual level. In turn, these objectives are translated into annual strategies and then detailed marketing tactics or programmes of activities. The logical consistency runs through both plans. Each of the marketing mix elements will now be discussed, with a particular focus on communications.

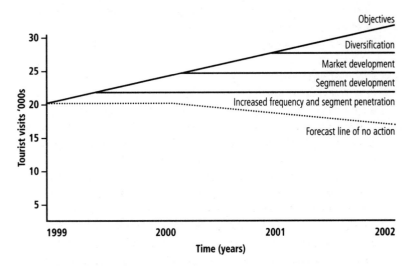

Figure 7.3: Strategic Gap Analysis

Product

Any destination needs to decide which combination of product strategies, integrated with the rest of the marketing mix, will best meet the strategic marketing objectives set (see Table 7.2). Strategy options may be reviewed by the local destination in the light of:

♦ **the destination life-cycle**. Like a human life, a destination will move through a series of stages from introduction to the marketplace, growth (rapidly increasing revenue from tourists), maturity (a slow-down in revenue growth accompanied by an increase in competition), decline (a fall in visitor numbers and revenue) and possible rejuvenation or relaunch. The types of tourist visiting the destination may vary by cycle stage. Different product offers or tourism components within the destination may be at different stages of the life-cycle.

♦ **the product portfolio**. Simply stated, destinations should try to assess all the product offers in terms of the relationship between revenue produced and resources absorbed, the overall size and growth rates of the appropriate tourist market and, where possible, the relative market share compared to close competitors. This information can help decisions about which product offers to develop and which to cull or discourage in order to achieve a balanced portfolio of products in the medium to long term.

♦ **relevant gaps** in either the product lines and/or the product length and depth for a particular line. A destination product line is a category of products offering either similar benefits or positioning, for example, an events/festival line or a 'white-knuckle' adventure line. Product lines can be widened by adding a new product line, for example, by adding a famous personality (real and mythical) line to the above. A product line can be lengthened by adding products to an existing line, for example, medieval *son et lumière* events to the existing events of agricultural shows, weekly markets, beer-drinking festival, etc. Product lines can be deepened by adding additional product items to existing products, for example, increasing the number of caves open to the public from two to four, or by increasing *son et lumière* events from one site to five. Conversely, product lines, products and product items can also be rationalized.

♦ *analysis of tourist satisfaction* with each product offer in terms of benefits sought, key choice criteria, individual product attributes rated by the tourist as important, and scoring of associated satisfaction levels against close competitors.

♦ *development of product differentiation* relevant to the target market and distinct from competitors. Can the distinctive competencies and strengths identified be used to build long-term advantage? A unique selling proposition?

Table 7.3 illustrates three possible product strategies for the longer time period, and how these strategies then logically translate into the annual product objectives and strategies. Naturally, creativity is the source of success, and the choices at each successive level are numerous. A marketing plan may consist of a large number of chosen strategies. Strategy level options may involve extending or rationalizing the product line, length or depth, improving product quality, improving environmental credentials, developing special interest packages, building the local identity in the destination product, strengthening the destination image, developing new attractions (or any other tourism component), renovating mature product offers, improving products for resident use, and so forth.

Examples of product strategies 3 year
- develop products to increase destination y's season through events in the shoulder months and improving all-weather or undercover activities
- co-operate with destination z to expand the total market by developing joint product offers
- improve the aesthetic environment of destination y (secondary target residents)

Examples of product objectives 1 year
- launch two events/festivals for tourists, one in May 2000 and one in October 2000
- pilot a themed scenic drive unifying the two destinations in a circuit tour for testing in June 2000
- introduce three resident-driven initiatives to improve the overall appearance of destination y by December 2000

Examples of product strategies 1 year
- develop the existing May livestock show to appeal to tourists and to launch a new 'living arts' festival in October
- develop the culinary theme of spice production, trade and use in the combined area, with a focus on small holdings with visitor potential for spice production, markets selling spices, local restaurants and and accommodation specializing in spice use and the forthcoming (2001) spice visitor centre
- harness local youth groups to renovate the main entrance and exit points as part of their fund-raising campaigns, launch destination y's 'best garden' award in conjunction with the gardeners' association, and to introduce a 'sponsored litter bin' scheme amongst local businesses

---

Table 7.3: Illustrative Product Objectives and Strategies

'People' may also be thought of as part of the destination product when viewed from a marketing perspective. Customer care training (see Chapter 8), language, health and hygiene training may aid incremental product improvement. Motivation and award schemes linked to tourist satisfaction could be introduced. On the opposite side of the equation, how might tourist behaviour be influenced beneficially?

The product tactics map out the essential detail for implementing the product decisions. A Gantt chart may be used to break down discrete actions with timings and responsibilities attached (see Table 7.4).

Activity	Time periods, e.g. months or weeks												Responsibility	Budget £s
	1	2	3	4	5	6	7	8	9	10	11	12		
Identify main entry/ exit points	|—|												Mrs 'J'	0
Initial meetings with youth groups	|——|												Mrs 'J' & youth groups	0
Analysis & agreement of work required			|——|										Committee & youth groups	0
Donation of materials from DIY store	|————|												Mr 'C'	£500
Work on entry/exit points			|——————————|										Youth groups	0
Publicity for project		|—————————————————|											Mrs 'S'	£300
Unveiling dinner etc.											|—|		Mrs 'J' & youth groups	£200

Table 7.4: Example of a Simple Gantt Chart

Price

The marketing mix element over which a local destination has little control (assuming no regulatory powers), compared to the individual tourism supplier. Nonetheless, price is important for the destination marketing plan because it:

♦ *directly influences revenue obtained*, and can be used to manipulate number of visits and even length of stay according to the marketing objectives set;

♦ *signals product quality* to the tourist, helping to establish expectation levels and resultant satisfaction;

♦ *is flexible* and can trigger an immediate response in demand (see sales promotions);

♦ *is easy to copy* and can leave a destination vulnerable to price wars if the destination fails to build product differentiation and local identity;

♦ *refers to costs* from a tourist perspective and may, therefore, include effort, time spent, uncertainty and risks (financial, temporal and psychological) associated with the decision to visit.

In general, with due reference to the tourist segments targeted, a local destination is best advised to encourage a full range of prices amongst the total number of different tourism components. Destination prices are too often decided on a competitive-parity basis, as local destinations find it hard to escape from the trap of neighbouring competitors' prices. However, it is preferable to relate prices to the value perceived by tourist segments, their sensitivity to price changes and to the desired positioning in the target's mind. Generally, a tourist who has paid substantial amounts of money to arrive at the destination is less price sensitive to individual tourism components (one obvious exception being the backpacker taking a 'year out' to travel).

On the surface, it appears that there is little that the destination itself can do with regard to prices. Pricing is the concern of participating organizations and businesses. Yet consider the following points that might require co-operation, negotiation, or even fall outside the pricing decisions of individuals:

♦ Is there a common policy towards residents in the destination regarding access to tourist facilities that they might rightly regard as theirs? Free access on production of identity? Free or reduced price access at off-peak times? Residents may have guests staying (VFR travel) and can be encouraged to bring these visitors frequently if there is no additional cost to themselves. A 'friends of destination x' scheme with certain privileges can be an asset.

♦ Is there a common policy towards tourist and / or resident groups less able to afford access? Unemployed? Retired?

contd

Students? Discounts should be 'fenced' with clear rules regarding eligibility and acceptable identification of status to avoid revenue dilution.

♦ Pricing, if any, of amenities such as car parking or public lavatories.

♦ Development of pricing schemes to support the environment. For example, voluntary percentage donated to a trust, discounts for tourists arriving by public transport, tourist taxes (if legally viable), or voluntary parking charges.

♦ Combination ticket prices of a temporary or permanent nature, either between components within the local destination or between two or more local destinations. All inclusive price? Discount structure? Multi-visit? Added value in addition to price? Tailored to which tourist segments? For which time periods?

♦ Voluntary pricing policies for not-for-profit attractions and activities, perhaps using donation, honesty or special project appeal boxes.

♦ Negotiating with incoming tour operators as a group for more favourable trade prices? Commission rates to distributors such as TICs or travel agents?

♦ Computerized destination management systems, which act as reservation systems for a local destination. Pricing parameters? Time booked in advance, including last-minute bookings? Method of payment? The system captures tourist data that can feed back into the intelligence-gathering process for decision-making.

Table 7.5 illustrates three examples of possible destination pricing strategies. They are more oriented towards group schemes and encouragement of common policies than the traditional pricing strategies of individual businesses directly controlling price setting. Gantt charts for required activities, timings and responsibilities can be designed as for the product example shown before (see Table 7.4).

Examples of pricing strategies 3 year

- co-operate with destination to expand total market by agreeing mutually beneficial pricing schemes
- develop pricing schemes to assist in environmental improvement
- encourage resident (and their guests) use of tourist attractions and amenities, particularly in the off-peak period

---

Examples of pricing objectives 1 year

- test market a combined attractions ticket offering 40% discount plus added value during June 2000
- £1 voluntary contribution per person to be suggested addition to accommodation bills for conservation project x. To raise £10,000 between January and December 2000
- achieve 80% of attractions and activities offering either free entry to residents (guests full price) or at least 50% discount to residents (guests full price) at off-peak times by December 2000

Examples of pricing strategies 1 year

- combined attractions ticket to bring together voluntary participants (attractions and activities) on the 'heroes and villains' themed route valid for 7 consecutive days from the date of purchase and targeted at the independent family drive market
- establish a trust fund for project x with monitoring and visible publication and dissemination of results
- persuade potential participants that, as shown by 1998 research, additional VFR business gained outweighs 'lost' resident revenue. Recruitment drive with group presentations and personal meetings

---

Table 7.5: Illustrative Pricing Objectives and Strategies

Distribution

Distribution channels or pipelines are 'routes of exchange' through which a tourist accesses, books, confirms and pays for a tourism product. Intermediaries or distributors that might be involved in a pipeline include tourist information centres, national or regional tourist boards, incoming tour operators, wholesalers, overseas tour operators, travel agencies, special interest groups, bus/coach/ferry/airline/cruise ship operators, car-hire companies, incentive travel firms, meeting and conference planners, satisfied tourists, and so on. Essentially, a destination can choose from two strategic options:

◆ **Adopt an intensive** (maximum number of outlets), **selective or exclusive** (small number of outlets) **distribution strategy regarding outlet types and numbers**. Those local destinations with a luxury or premium positioning may adopt an exclusive distribution strategy, selecting outlets enhancing their positioning. Most local destinations would opt for a selective or intensive distribution strategy within the confines of resource constraints to maximize potential tourist access. Of course, individual product offers may prefer different strategies so that, in practice, a mix emerges for the destination as a whole.

♦ **Adopt a push or a pull strategy.** A push strategy focuses on distribution outlets urging them to sell to the tourist, while a pull strategy is directed at generating tourism demand which is then sucked through the appropriate distribution outlets. Closely associated with communications strategy, most local destinations use a combination of the two.

Individual tourism businesses have their own distribution channels, and the involvement of the destination itself will vary from a facilitating or top-up role to more active engagement. The following points should be discussed:

♦ **Portfolio of distribution channels.** What types of distribution channel are currently used? Numbers in each type? Cost of servicing the channel versus revenue produced? Used by which tourist segments? Suited to domestic or international business? Cross-comparison for early bookings, last-minute bookings and off-peak bookings?

♦ **Potential for channel conflict.** Each intermediary has its own objectives, which may not coincide with those of the destination. Where is the balance of power between the local destination and its intermediaries? Local destinations often have less power than many of the intermediaries. Maintenance or development of a balanced portfolio of a variety of distribution channels that avoids dependency on one particular type could be a wise decision.

♦ **Overlaps with communications.** Many communication tools in tourism can and do double as distribution channels. Check that contact name, address and telephone number and/or e-mail and web site addresses are included on advertisements, brochures and leaflets, sales promotions, backs of postcards, etc. Attention should also be given to letter-writing skills and telephone behaviour (see Chapter 8) so that responses are professionally handled. Communication is a two-way process. A database can catch the information for subsequent use.

♦ **Opportunities for co-operation** in distribution with nearby destinations, serving to stretch limited resources further.

♦ **Opportunities in electronic distribution**, such as web sites, that may be particularly relevant for independent international tourists in higher socio-economic groups.

♦ **Physical distribution and monitoring of print**. Some destinations use tourism trade fairs, travel brochure swap shops organized by tourist boards, the TIC network, libraries, garages, dentists' and doctors' surgeries, direct mail to previous tourists or enquirers, special interest groups, clubs and societies, regionally based businesses and factories, special events related to the destination, car-hire outlets, retail outlets, and so on. If brochures and leaflets are coded and tourists asked, the rough cost/revenue profiles for print outlet types can be monitored to guide future decisions.

Table 7.6 illustrates three examples of possible destination distribution strategies. Gantt charts for required activities, timings and responsibilities can be prepared as shown previously in Table 7.4.

Examples of distribution strategies 3 year

• reduce dependency on large tour operators and coach operators based outside the country
• increase the number of outlets good at generating off-peak business
• rationalize the numbers and types of destination outlets used according to cost-revenue profiles

---

Examples of distribution objectives 1 year

• reduce the % of business from the dominant three-coach and large tour operators from 50% to 40% by December 2000 without detriment to local businesses
• increase outlet type a from 15 to 25 and outlet type b from 5 to 15 by December 2000
• decrease leaflet outlet type c from 20 to top 3, and remove all leaflet outlet types d and e by December 2000

Examples of distribution strategies 1 year

• dual strategy of increasing independent travel and specialist package operators, plus renegotiation of contracts with dominant 3 tour and coach operators
• recruit outlets type a and b that best match existing successful outlets in (a) existing main generating markets for off-peak business (b) the 2 leading growth markets for off-peak business where the destination has no current presence
• final monitoring of leaflet outlet performance during peak season, adjustment of database and roll-out culling programme from September to December with explanation

---

Table 7.6: Illustrative Distribution Objectives and Strategies

FOCUS ON COMMUNICATIONS

The final element of the marketing mix to be introduced here is communications, the tool for achieving objectives, so often confused with marketing itself. Informal communication occurs every time a resident meets a tourist through appearance, words and body language (see Chapter 8). It is easier, of course, for destination marketers to control the formal communication tools; in essence, advertising, public relations, sales promotions, personal selling and print. The combination of these tools makes up the basic communications mix. If required, separate plans can be drawn up for each of the communication tools, covering target audience, objectives, strategy, tactics, and evaluation and control, including the budget.

Three introductory points pertinent to the communications task for local destinations should be noted:

♦ Increasingly, local destinations are adopting a facilitating role for their individual providers. The production of shell leaflets for different businesses to adapt, or the negotiation of banner advertisements in newspapers using a destination logo under which individuals buy their space, are both examples.

♦ Communication campaigns should be integrated, so that different communication tools are used to support each other for maximum benefit. Sales promotions can be supported by advertising and advertising by public relations. Sponsorship needs the support and spin-off from a preplanned communications programme if opportunities are not to be wasted.

♦ Opportunities for joint communications campaigns with tourism components, other destinations, or even complementary physical goods or services should be pursued. Tourist boards at a national or regional level may also offer opportunities as part of their own facilitating role.

The link between the three points is the reality of financial resource constraint for local destinations using communications; all three help to stretch a minimal budget.

Target Audience

Tourist segments form the most obvious target audiences, but there are other stakeholder groups with which the destination may need to communicate. Additional target audiences might include the travel trade, media, financial sector, local and national government, tourist boards, business communities, resident groups, employees, pressure groups, other industries impacting on tourism in the area, and so on. As part of the profile of the target audience, media habits need to be understood if the audience is to be reached through communications.

The communications process is often described as a two-step process, with opinion leaders intervening between the destination and its potential tourists. Opinion leaders may be heavy users of tourism products, or frequent users, or those swift to try new tourism products; identification of these people and the media required to access them can improve the communication process. Destinations should realize that residents and workers within its boundaries form a secondary audience for all communications targeted at external audiences. Over-promising and misrepresentation in advertising has led marketing to be berated by local communities resenting the images portrayed. Such advertising is not motivating for the internal audience.

The AIDA model suggests that tourists move through *Attention* (awareness), to *Interest*, to *Desire* and, finally, to *Action*. An understanding about the target audiences' awareness and knowledge of the destination, feelings, beliefs and attitudes towards the destination, and behaviour connected with the destination, drives successful communications. It is no good communicating a special offer of a two day mini-break if the target audience have a negative attitude towards the destination itself, or are uninformed about what is has to offer.

Communication Objectives
Different communication tools are better at achieving different communication objectives. Broadly speaking, advertising and public relations are good at building awareness and interest, while sales promotions and personal selling are good at building desire and action. Communication objectives may include:

♦ increasing awareness, interest, desire or action in the target audience, or by moving the target audience from one stage to the next;

♦ strengthening or changing destination image or positioning;

♦ depositioning a competing destination or altering its image;

contd

- persuading the target audience of the benefits of the destination;

- changing the relative importance of buying criteria, e.g. reducing the perceived importance of price in decision-making;

- regaining public confidence in the aftermath of a crisis, e.g. a food scare, mugging, or natural disaster;

- generating prospects for visiting the destination;

- including the destination amongst the set of possible choices from which the final decision to visit is made;

- improving conversion rates from print pick-up rates through to enquiries through to bookings;

- shifting buyer behaviour patterns according to seasonality or by the time lag between purchase and use;

- encouraging trial use in the target audience;

- launching a new product offer, or relaunching an existing product, within the destination;

- stimulating additional purchase, perhaps relating to length of stay;

- prompting repeat usage;

- developing word-of-mouth recommendation to boost referred business;

- reassuring tourists experiencing post-purchase anxiety of the soundness of their decision;

- reminding potential repeat tourists about the destination;

- changing tourist behaviour patterns at the destination, perhaps in respect of negative impacts.

The list is not exhaustive, but illustrative. Like the marketing objectives, the communications objectives agreed need to be stated in a format that is specific, timed and measurable. An example might be 'to raise awareness of destination X amongst American ABC1 couples repeat visiting in the UK from 5% in June 2000 to 25% in June 2001'.

Communication Strategies

These summarize the mix of communication tools – advertising, public relations, sales promotions, personal selling and print, outlining how each will be used in the plan. To arrive at these strategies, each of the main communications tools is now examined by turn.

Advertising: Defined as non-personal, paid for, mass communication by an identified sponsor in a commercially available medium. In this case, the sponsor is the local destination and any partners involved in the campaign. An advertising agency offers skilled creative work plus advantageous rates for purchasing media space; even a destination with a small budget should weigh up the benefits of employing an agency. Table 7.7 outlines the main media available for advertising destinations.

Media type	Comment
• Press: newspapers	National/regional/local; daily/weekend; paid for/free; broadsheet/tabloid. Opportunities for inserts? Newspaper supplements? Special editions?
• Press: magazines	Lifestyle, gender-based, professional, special interest. Opportunities for inserts? Special editions?
• Tourism print	Guidebooks, tourist board brochures/trade manuals, local govt. print, travel trade magazines, national park papers, airline inflight magazines/other component equivalent
• Videos	Inflight videos, tourist board videos, movie videos for rent
• Billboards/posters	Outdoor sites, transport stops and stations, vehicles (taxis, buses, trams, airport trolleys, etc.)
• Radio	National/local; commercial/government
• Web sites	Banner advertisements, screen savers, placing links at other sites
• Cinema	Prohibitively expensive (unless joint campaign)
• Television	Prohibitively expensive (unless joint campaign)
• Unusual	Floor posters, ceiling posters, parking tickets, petrol pumps, ariel banners, balloon (display or release), golf balls & tees, food and drink packaging associated with area, etc.

Table 7.7: Advertising Media for Destinations

As a rough guide, of the total advertising budget, typically only 10–15% is spent on creative and production costs, with 85–90% being earmarked for purchasing space in appropriate media vehicles. Television and cinema may be prohibitively expensive for a local destination to consider, quite apart from the relevance of the audience. If a destination were to examine its advertising spend in the context of total advertising spend on travel and tourism, it would discover that it had a minute 'share of voice' in the market. Consequently, only creative advertising whose results are monitored will make that spend worthwhile.

In choosing the desired media, the destination should think through:

♦ *audience size and type* and the fit to the profile of the destination's target audience, using information provided by the media vehicles themselves or by an independent body.

♦ *audience mood* and receptivity to message at the time when the advertisement is seen and/or heard. Relaxed? Concentrated? Happy? Contemplative? Pressed for time?

♦ *cost of production* and cost of space for series of advertisements. Media vehicles produce rate cards of prices which can then be used to compare costs across different vehicles on a cost per thousand of target audience basis.

♦ *advantages and disadvantages* for message communication with regard to sight, sound, movement, colour, reproduction, ability to convey information and/or image, ability to refer back versus transitory nature, etc.

♦ *process of buying media space* regarding lead times, deadlines, legal approval process (if required), danger of loss of space to higher bidder, etc.

The media buyer needs to calculate the amount of space required, the position of the advertisement, frequency of insertion or equivalent and timing. A drip strategy places advertisements consistently through time, while a burst strategy concentrates advertising for a set time period, sometimes following up with a second burst later.

Alongside the media planning is the creative planning, which focuses on the message itself, tone of voice required, its translation into creative concepts, evaluation of creative concepts using the target audience, development into the full advertisement, additional testing and, finally, production. If working with an advertising agency, a destination will expect to sign off key stages to give approval to ideas. Someone will need to take responsibility for the finished advertisements arriving at each media vehicle by the deadlines. The tactical Gantt chart can look quite complex.

Public Relations: Defined as the planned and sustained effort to establish and maintain goodwill and mutual understanding between a destination and its publics (adapted from the UK Institute of Public Relations). Good public relations is about credibility, not about papering over the cracks. Public relations, or PR, is increasing in popularity with destinations, partly due to the intrinsic nature of tourism lending itself to newsworthy stories and partly due to the rising costs of purchasing advertising space. Handled professionally, PR can create awareness, interest, understanding, and information at a fraction of the cost of advertising. Public relations can be used to target a wide range of audiences, apart from the tourist segments. Table 7.8 highlights the main PR tools and techniques available to a destination.

Tools and techniques	Comment
• Publicity & media relations	Generating publicity and media coverage through database of media contacts, press releases, feature articles, photocalls, press conferences, press interviews, journalist visits, press packs & photographic library
• Product placement	Negotiating for destination use in film, television, advertisements, radio, etc.
• Familiarization trips	For intermediaries, opinion leaders, other target audiences
• Product launches and staged events or stunts	Based around new products, product relaunches, personality appearances, special events focused around a story, launch of a communications campaign
• Exhibitions	Trade/public; stands at conferences and meetings, travel fairs, workshops, etc.
• Sponsorship	Either as a sponsor of the community, arts, sports, education, media or unusual vehicle, and/or as a sponsoree with a portfolio of opportunities for others to sponsor. Joint sponsorship opportunities? Be wary of any potential for competitors to ambush the planned sponsorship programme.
• Public speaking	Lectures, conferences & workshops, speeches, presentations, guest 'expert' for local media, etc.
• Corporate identity	For destination; consistency in logo, letterheads, styling and colour, signage, maps, leaflets, etc.
• Crisis management	Rehearsed scenarios for dealing with natural/man-made disaster, blackmail-type threats, crisis real or perceived as real by target audience
• Internal communication	Briefing individuals representing destination, internal meetings, community newsletters, public noticeboards, etc.

Table 7.8: Public Relations Tools and Techniques for Destinations

As a newsworthy product, a destination has similar advantages for product placement and as a subject for external sponsorship. Conversely, it is vulnerable to unpredictable man-made or natural events, emphasizing the necessity for good crisis management.

Public relations is also involved with developing the credibility of the destination. Issues such as environmental credentials, customer satisfaction, product quality and ethical issues are all related to credibility. Raising visibility through PR before building credibility is one short cut to self-inflicted crises.

Sales Promotions: Defined as any temporary, short-term incentive designed to stimulate some kind of action in the target audience. Broadly speaking, the target audience consists of:

♦ key tourist segments;

♦ intermediaries and distribution outlets;

♦ internal audiences, such as residents, workers, local businesses etc., requiring motivation.

Well-conceived sales promotions are excellent at:

♦ boosting trial usage;

♦ generating extra usage in shoulder or trough months (weeks/days/hours etc.);

♦ increasing frequency and/or volume of use.

Some sales promotions, such as discounted prices, have an immediate effect, while others, such as competitions, have a delayed effect. Table 7.9 outlines the main sales promotions techniques open to a destination, subject to the varying legal restrictions, country to country, governing its use. According to Middleton (1988), an important distinction should be made between those sales promotions based on discounted price and those based on added value; added value may be the superior proposition where destinations are trying to move away from price comparison. Certainly, all destinations should assess sales promotions in the context of the effect on their image and positioning, even though this is unlikely to be cited as an objective for the tool.

Type of sales promotion	Comment or example
• Reduced prices	£2 off third night from 1–30 Nov. 2000
• Discount vouchers and coupons (from direct mail, newspaper ad., flyer, etc.)	10% discount for attraction entry on presentation of voucher from 1–30 Nov. 2000.
• Disguised price cut	First child goes free from 1–30 Nov. 2000
• Added value of physical good or service	Free bottle of local wine on arrival from 1–30 Nov. 2000. Check relevance of added value to target audience.
• Buy two and get one free	Buy two full-priced adult entry tickets and get third free between 1–30 Nov. 2000
• Competitions, prize draws and sweepstakes	Complete the sentence in no more than 12 words: 'My family visits destination x because ... '
• Charity promotion	On each accommodation night per person between 1–30 Nov. 2000, participating suppliers will donate 50p to charity x
• Self-liquidating premium	Tourist posts one or more proofs of purchase, e.g. two tickets plus money and receives destination video/T-shirt/ local craft object, etc. Calculate and monitor take-up rates
• Free premium	Tourist posts in one or more proofs of purchase and receives destination video, etc. free
• Refund offer	Tourist sends in one or more proofs of purchase and receives refund of fixed amount, e.g. £3
• Override commissions	Intermediaries receive additional commission, e.g. extra 5% on each sale made between 1–30 Nov. 2000
• Point of purchase displays	Displays in distribution outlets, windows or by service point
• Merchandising	Giveaways or for sale items carrying destination message or or logo, e.g. T-shirts, etc. For intermediaries or consumers

Table 7.9: Sales Promotions for Destinations

Personal Selling: Defined as oral communication between one or more prospective purchasers and a salesperson for the purpose of making a sale. There are two main categories of this personal form of communication for a destination:

♦ communication through every encounter between a destination resident or worker and a tourist (see Chapter 8). A tourist may experience hundreds of such encounters each day, and some may present an opportunity to make an additional sale. For example, the waiter enquiring after desserts or coffee, the barman checking drinks, etc.;

♦ face-to-face conversation between a destination representative and a high-value customer, whether or not they are the end-user.

Personal selling in the latter case is an expensive communications tool best used where the individual prospect can bring high-value business to the destination. Individual targets may include meeting and conference organizers, incentive travel organizers, large tour operators or coach companies, special interest groups and so on. Personal selling is as much about retaining such customers and building a strong relationship with them through client servicing as it is about winning the initial business. Representatives also feed back useful information on external trends or on competitor activity.

Tourism Print: This includes brochures, leaflets, postcards, business cards, maps, codes of conduct, timetables and tickets. They are all tangible clues about the tourism experience and they may be designed to:

♦ create or strengthen an image or positioning for the destination;

♦ give information about the destination;

♦ package together separate components of accommodation, attractions, activities, excursions, etc. in a fixed or flexible format;

♦ act as a purchasing device through, for example, a booking form or sales promotion coupon;

♦ minimize post-purchase anxiety by providing tangible reassurance after a booking has been made;

♦ alter tourist behaviour to minimize negative physical and socio-cultural impacts at the destination;

♦ facilitate tourist use of the destination, perhaps influencing patterns of usage or increasing length of stay.

(adapted from Middleton, 1988)

The use of colour, photographs of the target audience using the destination, line drawings, typeface, density and style of text, thickness and quality of paper all relay messages about the destination to the tourist. These messages should support rather than undermine the destination image.

Destinations should also discuss print distribution issues before producing the print, for example, total weight for mailings and related postage prices, or size, layout and positioning on racks for maximum visibility. If production costs are an issue, the shelf life of a piece of print can be prolonged by inserting current prices on a loose sheet of paper that is cheap to update.

Coding print by outlet can assist with monitoring, and all print should carry contact information. Print should be co-ordinated with a corporate or destination style; much destination print consists of a motley collection of one-off productions that does little to enhance the destination's positioning over time. The downside of print is that the marketplace is cluttered with tourism and leisure contributions, and conversion rates from tourist pick up to usage are small. Creativity, attention to print objectives, and precise targeting are essential for print success.

Other Communication Tools: These may also be incorporated into the communications mix. Of the formal tools under the control of the destination, the design of web sites and the use of direct marketing campaigns drawing on information captured on databases can be very worthwhile for local destinations. Information can be collected from previous tourists, enquiries, sales promotions campaigns, direct response advertisements, destination print, and so on. Lists may be bought in from other organizations, or taken from published sources, such as *Yellow Pages*. Geodemographic tools, where available, may be used to locate other prospects with matching profiles. The key to success in direct marketing is to target tightly.

Word of mouth is a form of communication not controlled by the destination, yet it is highly influential to the success of the area's tourism. As bad word of mouth spreads faster than positive recommendation, attention to customer care and to quality is vital (see Chapter 8).

The focus on communications ends the review of the marketing mix. Decisions about the marketing mix allows the destination to answer the question 'how do we get there?' It is then necessary to move on to the final question of the marketing process, namely 'how do we know if we've got there?'

HOW DO WE KNOW IF WE'VE GOT THERE?

Simply stated, a destination needs to check that its objectives have been achieved. An additional question could quite legitimately be tacked on to the classic question of 'how do we know if we've got there?' In short, 'how do we make sure that we get there?' This stage of the marketing process is all about evaluation, monitoring and control:

♦ **Evaluation** is the periodic assessment at the end of a marketing plan to check whether objectives were indeed achieved. A marketing audit or in-depth review can provide a very thorough assessment of performance.

♦ **Monitoring** is the ongoing systematic measurement of performance. It compares actual results against the translated objectives into daily, weekly and monthly targets. It therefore allows for gaps in performance to be spotted early on and for corrective action to be taken.

♦ **Control** is the tactical activity carried out to close the gaps between actual performance and daily, weekly or monthly targets identified by monitoring. It can only be done after an analysis of the cause of the performance shortfall, for example, unforeseen competitor activity or unusual weather patterns. To be effective, control may require preplanned contingency actions and access to a contingency budget labelled for such eventualities.

Gantt charts as recommended under tactics can provide a map of order, timings and responsibilities for discrete activities. The marketing activities will require human input (*men*), financial input (*money*) and time (*minutes*). The fourth M of *measurement* allows the use of these resources to be monitored for their productivity.

The budget is the sum of the costs of all the activities judged necessary for meeting objectives, plus a percentage as a contingency budget. Budget setting is best achieved through an objective and task method, where the costs of tasks are related to the objective set. The budget is then split between the different marketing mix components. The budget is usually expressed within the text of the marketing plan in actual terms and as a percentage of tourist revenue.

In monitoring performance, destinations should consider how best to use:

♦ **destination records** of number of visits, tourist expenditure, number of nights, length of stay, activity patterns, etc. Comparison of such internal data against weekly and monthly targets can aid the identification of any gaps in performance.

♦ **variance and trends** in customer satisfaction from ongoing surveys.

- *before-and-after research* to examine changes in attitude, feelings, destination images and so on, using surveys and focus groups both before and after a communications campaign.

- *marketing productivity ratios*, both as a trend over time and as a variance to any objectives set. The ratios of outputs to inputs, for example, the revenue produced by a particular distribution channel to the costs of servicing it, the number of enquiries generated to the costs of advertising in a particular media vehicle, the number of hits on a web site to the costs of establishing and maintaining the site and so on.

- *key marketing indicators*, which can be traced over time. Examples include the mean advertising cost per visit, the mean communications cost per visit, the conversion rates for different forms of print and so on.

For monitoring performance, some forms of data will be collected from existing records, although methods may need adjustment to ensure that the right type of information is captured. Other data will require specific research tailored to the specific problem. Chapter 9 explores research in greater detail. Co-operation of individual tourism businesses in collating destination records is recommended but fallible. Individual operators are sometimes reluctant to relinquish data considered competitively sensitive. The destination should not rely on such information to monitor performance and should develop alternatives over which it has greater control, for example, records of visits to the local TIC.

Referring back to Table 7.1 (page 126) should show how the framework of the marketing plan has progressed, and how it answers the four classic questions posed in the introduction. Naturally, the process of marketing rolls over from one set of plans to the next, with monitoring and evaluation feeding into subsequent rounds of decision-making.

WHERE TO NEXT?

This chapter has examined the development of the destination marketing plan, stressing that the local destination needs to make improvements in many areas rather than relying on a single 'big idea' breakthrough. While appreciating the wider remit of marketing, the communications mix was given special treatment. One of the additional areas that merits attention from all local destinations is that of customer care, destination welcome and customer satisfaction, which are sometimes collectively referred to as *destination hospitality*. It is this topic that Chapter 8 will address.

FURTHER READING *for Developing the Marketing Plan*

McDonald, M. (1995) *Marketing plans. How to prepare them: how to use them* (3rd edition). Oxford: Butterworth-Heinemann.

Middleton, V.T.C. (1994) *Marketing in travel and tourism* (2nd edition). Oxford: Butterworth-Heinemann.

World Tourism Organization (1997) *Shining in the media spotlight*. Madrid: WTO (good directory of key media contacts relevant for tourism).

World Tourism Organization (1998) *Travel and Tourism Fairs*. Madrid: WTO (practical advice for participating in tourism trade fairs).

CHAPTER EIGHT

Keeping the tourist
Destination welcome and customer care

INTRODUCTION

In the globally competitive marketplace, attention to every detail of the tourism product and the tourist visit repays the time and effort spent. It is not enough to be good in one or two areas; to compete, a tourism destination needs to offer a total quality experience. This simple fact is sometimes overlooked by local destinations, who tend to focus on providing accommodation to the detriment of attractions, activities and support services. Close attention to the detail as explained in this chapter can help to:

♦ increase tourist satisfaction with the experience;

♦ increase the length of stay in the locality where flexibility is a characteristic of the tourist (see Chapter 5);

♦ generate positive word-of-mouth recommendation which boosts referred business;

♦ encourage repeat visits from previously satisfied tourists;

♦ differentiate the local destination from competitors over the longer term.

Gaining visits from new tourists is an expensive option as this involves either expanding the market or diverting business from competitors. Repeat visits and referred visits are much more cost-effective. As a guideline, it costs five to ten times less to keep an existing tourist than it does to replace one. Any destination should strive to fulfil the potential of retained and referred business. Ideally, a healthy balance between new, referred and repeat business should be sought, and a destination would be wise to monitor the trends in these types of custom (see Table 8.1).

Business	% 2000	% 2001	% 2002	% 2003	% etc.
New					
Referred					
Repeat					
Total	100	100	100	100	100

Table 8.1: The Balance of Destination Business

This chapter, in following the remit of attention to detail regarding the tourism product and tourist visit, touches on many different topics and issues. The topics are equally applicable to a single tourism organization or business and to the tourism destination. The most noticeable difference is that the individual tourism organization, particularly those operating in the commercial sector, will have immediate control over decision-making and resulting action. The tourism destination, however, will need to rely on persuasion and co-operation to achieve similar things. This chapter adopts the perspective of the tourism destination.

Binding together the many different topics and issues are five key themes. These are highlighted in Figure 8.1 (page 161), and will resurface throughout the chapter. To be influential, these five key themes need to be embedded in a framework that locks together strategy, people and processes. Some initial explanation of the five key themes is required:

♦ **tourist focus** – creating tourist satisfaction is paramount to achieving destination goals; the tourist must be placed at the centre of activity. The process of selecting tourist segments has already ensured that only those types of tourist beneficial in achieving destination goals are encouraged (see Chapter 5), so the focus of attention on these groups should not be misplaced. Activity is aided by the destination's understanding of the wants and needs of these groups. Within the segments, individual visitors must be made to feel special. Satisfaction with an experience occurs at the individual, rather than segment, level. Individuals vary by mobility, health, dietary requirements, size and shape and so forth. All have needs that must be catered for.

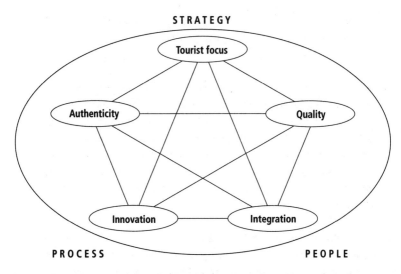

Figure 8.1: Five Key Themes for Keeping the Tourist

♦ **quality** – this is typically misunderstood as being upmarket for good quality and downmarket for poor quality, for example, a luxury hotel being high quality and a campsite being poor quality. This is not true. Quality in tourism is concerned with consistency and reliability; it is about satisfying the tourist 100% of the time. As satisfaction is based on expectations, both the luxury hotel and the campsite can be equally successful in attaining quality.

♦ **authenticity** – again, this is sometimes misunderstood as being an attempt to halt progress at a local destination, to turn the area into a museum-piece. In practice, authenticity is about identifying those social, cultural, economic and physical features that helped to create the special character of the area. The debate surrounding the use and abuse of authenticity in tourism is a complex one; however, authenticity can provide the basis for developing a unique identity for the destination in line with global trends. It is tricky for a competitor to copy features that are not typical outside of the area. With time, attention to building authenticity into the tourism product can help differentiate a destination from its competitors. All destinations should be aware that what may seem ordinary, even bordering on the forgettable, for inhabitants, may be of interest to the tourist. The may is stressed, for some destinations develop an inward focus on the product. A tourist-focus, or the ability to see things from the tourists' perspective, is vital.

♦ **innovation** – for medium- and long-term success, local destinations must continuously improve their product. Tourist expectations rise and competitors improve, so that the destination that stands still is liable to lose out. Innovation implies creative thought, but, although the single breakthrough idea is possible, development is more likely to be achieved by lots of small improvements in many areas. Destinations should analyse every aspect of the product, including the people and processes involved.

♦ **integration** – owners, managers and employees of the different tourism components must recognize their interdependence with one another, and co-operate to offer a seamless tourism experience to the visitor. In reality, rivalry will be apparent between commercial operators in the same sector, for example, amongst accommodation units of a particular class. However, the broader understanding that co-operation and integration helps to expand total business for the area should be appreciated. A spirit of co-operation should be nurtured. Likewise, every person in every facet of the local tourism industry, from hotel receptionist to taxi driver, tour guide to shopkeeper needs to understand their role in delivering the tourism experience.

Figure 8.1 also displays an outer ring consisting of *strategy*, *people* and *processes*. These provide the framework within which the key themes are located.

♦ **strategy** – the local destination needs to understand its mission, its goals and objectives, and its strategies for achieving these (see Chapters 6 and 7). Such an understanding creates a sense of direction for decision-making and facilitates integration between different people through a shared sense of purpose.

♦ **people** – tourism is a people-based experience rich in human contact. This creates differences between every tourist visit. Each one is unique. It is difficult to control quality when the human factor is so dominant. However, it is easy for a competitor to copy the physical features of a tourism product, but much harder to copy the people skills, motivation and ambience. The people involved in the tourism product are the tourist, the other tourists present at the same time and place who influence the individual's satisfaction with the experience, the contact staff who interact with the tourist, and the non-contact staff who never meet the tourist but who provide support services and processes. Of course, contact staff include those who work in the tourism industry, but also residents who meet tourists yet do not feel associated with the industry. Destinations should try to influence the behaviour of all these participants.

♦ **process** – these are the systems, or the ways of getting things done, that are used to deliver the tourism product. Processes may be computerized, partially computerized, or manual. Examples include reservation and booking systems, grading and classification systems, staff reward systems, complaint management systems, marketing research systems, and so on.

This chapter concentrates on strategies, people and processes. However, 'practical tips' are given in boxes to guide thoughts on operational practice. These are not intended to be comprehensive, but rather illustrative of the possibilities.

GETTING THE BEST FROM QUALITY

Quality for the tourism destination is primarily concerned with consistency and reliability in satisfying desirable tourists 100% of the time. In order to be satisfied, a tourist's perception of the experience received must equal or exceed the expectations held concerning that experience. Tourists judge both the process and the actual outcome. If perceptions fail to match expectations, dissatisfaction arises. This shortfall has been labelled as a *quality gap* (Parasuraman, Zeithaml and Berry, 1985). The quality gap is dynamic. The size of the gap will increase as tourist expectations increase, unless the destination uses continuous improvement as suggested to close the gap. Tourist expectations rise:

♦ with increasing experience of tourism products;

♦ with increasing standards of living in the home environment. For many tourism products, tourist segments expect an equal or greater standard of comfort than they experience at home;

- ◆ through comparison with other service sectors, such as retailing, where standards may be higher yet can be cross-compared against tourism, for example, queuing.

Parasuraman *et al.* (1985) identified types of quality gaps that could contribute to the overall gap between tourist perception and expectation. The three highlighted here are:

- ◆ the gap between the tourist's expectation of the experience and the destination's understanding of that expectation. This emphasizes the real importance of a tourist-focus. It also emphasizes the importance of marketing research.

- ◆ the gap between the design of the tourism product and the standards set, and the actual delivery of the tourism product. This may be caused by failure in any of the processes due to faulty equipment or human error, but it can also be triggered by poor human resource management.

- ◆ the gap between the perceived promises of communication campaigns and the actual tourism experience. Over-promising in advertising is rife in the tourism industry, yet exaggerated claims raise tourist expectations beyond the reality, leading to disappointment.

The destination tourism product is usually a customized experience that cannot be standardized across the total product (the exception being the inclusive resorts under single ownership). However, it is possible for certain aspects of the product to be standardized. Standards set should be tourist-driven; they should reflect expectations. Such tourist-defined standards become goals and guides for staff in performing tasks. Zeithaml and Bitner (1996) divide standards into:

- ◆ **hard standards**, or tourist-defined standards that can be counted, timed, observed in a structured manner, or otherwise quantified. Examples may include the number of days for a written response to a letter of enquiry or complaint, the number of seconds or minutes that elapse before a tourist is greeted upon entering an establishment, and the number of rings of a telephone before it is answered.

♦ **soft standards**, or tourist-defined standards cannot be measured by the methods used for hard standards. These are based on tourist opinion and can only be collected through marketing research. Examples include staff friendliness, courtesy, empathy, knowledge, ability to solve problems and tone of voice.

Figure 8.2 shows the process for establishing tourist-defined standards. The process relies on feedback mechanisms and marketing research (see Chapter 9). Research methods of relevance here are summarized in Table 8.2 (page 166). The results can be plotted on a matrix similar to the one shown in Figure 8.3 (page 167). This exercise is best conducted separately for the key tourist segments, and through time so that trends can be studied using a series of matrices. It is also possible to add the performance of competitors into the equation. An alternative way of tracking trends over time is shown in Figure 8.4 (page 167), where results are plotted against target levels. Discrepancies should be examined for underlying causes and the necessary corrective action taken.

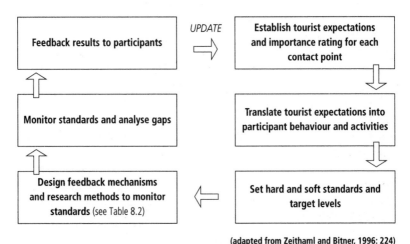

(adapted from Zeithaml and Bitner, 1996: 224)

Figure 8.2: Process for Establishing Tourist-defined Standards

STAGES OF THE TOURIST VISIT

Destinations are apt to focus on the tourist stay itself. However, from the tourist's perspective, a visit can be broken into five different stages as shown in Figure 8.5. The tourist has potential contact points with the destination at all of the five stages. Any of these contact points or encounters may result in tourist satisfaction or dissatisfaction and provide the tourist with an opportunity to judge the quality. There may be thousands of encounters attached to any one visit.

Some organizations map out, or blueprint, the entire chain of encounters, showing participants, activities, timings, bottlenecks, fail points and support activities invisible to the tourist. Blueprinting increases staff understanding of the product and aids continuous improvement by highlighting weaker areas. Again, it is important to develop this blueprint from the tourist's viewpoint. Some organizations conduct a blueprint for key segments and a blueprint for employees; the two are then compared for discrepancies.

Marketing research tool	Examples of uses
• Tourist surveys (by key segment)	To measure expectations and importance ratings To measure soft standards through opinion To monitor satisfaction levels and performance ratings To measure competitors' performance
• Staff/other participant surveys	To establish staff behaviour and activities To monitor satisfaction levels To identify common errors and fail points in processes
• Mystery shopping	To measure staff performance To measure competitors' performance To benchmark against better performing destinations/ establishments to improve product
• Focus groups	To explore range of expectations and opinions To discuss trends and changes in expectations
• Observation studies	To measure hard standards To measure staff performance To identify staff behaviour and activities
• Exit interviews and surveys	To identify reasons for tourist dissatisfaction To identify reasons for tourist defection to competitors
• Tourist panels	To monitor changing expectations, importance ratings and opinions through time
• Complaint solicitation	To identify and recover from negative incidents To identify patterns of errors and fail points
• Critical incident studies	To identify tourist expectations To identify common errors and fail points To analyse best practice at contact points
• Telephone trailer calls	To provide instant feedback on performance To assess individual staff performance

Table 8.2: Marketing Research Tools for Measuring Tourist-defined Standards

(adapted from Zeithaml and Bitner, 1996: 141)
NB Techniques can be used for other participants, such as staff and residents

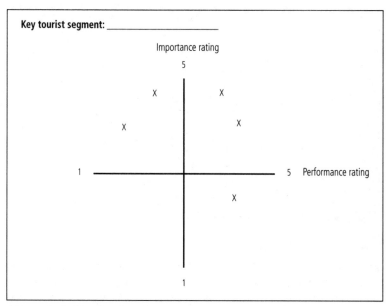

Figure 8.3: Plotting Results on a Matrix

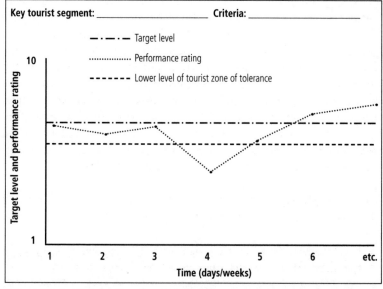

Figure 8.4: Plotting Results Over Time

Figure 8.5: Stages of the Tourist Visit

The Pre-visit Stage

Any local destination should pay attention to the pre-visit stage of the tourist experience, as this is the primary stage for the formation of expectations. Destinations can influence this process through communication campaigns and information provision (see Chapter 7). Overzealous promotion could result in expectations being set above what actually can be delivered.

Providing Clues: Usually, tourists cannot test the tourism experience before they purchase. They are likely to search for clues to help them establish their expectations. A high price indicates a high level of service, and a low price a low level of service. The latter is less useful, particularly with reference to the package-tour market, who may be attracted by low price but nonetheless have high expectations. The thickness and texture of the paper used in leaflets and brochures, the use of colour, line drawings and photographs, typeface, and so on, can also be used by the tourist as evidence. These physical clues should be planned and co-ordinated so that the messages conveyed are complementary rather than contradictory. Clues can also be used to stress individuality or to communicate the authenticity of the destination.

Personal Skills: The tourist's first indirect human encounter with the destination is likely to occur prior to arrival, through:

♦ **the telephone** (see Practical Tips for the Telephone, page 169);
♦ **the letter** (see Practical Tips for Letter Writing, page 169);
♦ **the Internet and electronic mail.**

Business can be won or lost on that initial encounter, and resources invested in destination development can be wasted if correspondence is not carried out professionally.

PRACTICAL TIPS FOR THE TELEPHONE

✓ Give the name of your organization when you greet the caller. It may be better to give your own name later in the conversation when they have time to absorb it.

✓ Smile on the phone – it helps to make your voice more enthusiastic and friendly.

✓ Use the caller's name where appropriate.

✓ Use open and closed questions.

✓ Check that the caller is satisfied with the outcome of the call before you finish.

✓ Let the caller replace the handset first – it sounds less abrupt.

✓ Keep a notebook and pen on a string by the phone and note the caller's name, number, the date and time, message, who took it and whom it was for. It is also useful to ask how they heard of you.

✓ Check that your outgoing message on the answer machine is professional. You should be aware that callers may hang up on hearing a recorded message and take their business elsewhere. An alternative telephone number may help.

✓ Allow the phone to ring more than three times; some people are disconcerted if it is picked up quickly as they need time to think of their opening sentence.

✓ However, if it takes time for the phone to be answered, for example, in a big house, advise potential callers to that effect in your promotional literature.

PRACTICAL TIPS FOR LETTER WRITING

✓ Set standards for response times to written correspondence.

✓ Design a filing system for all correspondence.

✓ Establish an appropriate 'atmosphere' for letters that reflects the identity of the product and is meaningful for the tourist. Letters are physical clues. Think about the letterhead, the thickness, colour and texture of the paper, the handwriting or typeface used, the envelope. Should the use of names be formal or informal?

✓ State dates, times, prices and contact methods and answer all questions asked.

✓ Is it appropriate to reply in the tourist's language? Keep a file of useful phrases if you feel that this develops your personal touch.

✓ Be aware of the weight of the letter and any enclosed information, as this may affect the postal charge. Know the postal price boundaries.

Reservation and Booking Systems: Individual businesses at the destination will develop reservation and booking systems as appropriate, but it is important to establish a destination system so that surplus business from any one establishment is redirected within the area (see the practical tips below). Some systems use computers and destination databases;

others are manual. Most are designed to top up existing business and to allocate 'spare' business.

PRACTICAL TIPS FOR DESTINATION & BOOKING SYSTEMS

✓ Issue establishments with a list of other establishments' names, addresses, phone numbers and relevant details.

✓ Publicize two central contact phone numbers in promotional literature as alternative choices for callers seeking neutral last-minute advice.

✓ Ensure that answer messages on contact phones are cross-referenced, so that if one is unavailable, the other number can be tried.

✓ Contact people may use a wall chart or reservation diary holding the details of other establishments.

✓ Make sure that the tourist information centre displays accommodation lists and a map outside the building, so that late arrivals can find accommodation even when the centre is closed. Police stations and transport stations are also useful places to display details.

✓ Some destinations operate a kitty so that establishments who receive bookings from a central contact point donate a fixed sum or % of the money. This goes towards joint advertising or leaflet production.

The Arrival Stage

The journey to the destination is part of the total experience, yet it is one that may leave the tourist in an unfavourable frame of mind upon arrival (tired, hot, sweaty, thirsty, etc.). The arrival occupies only a fraction of the entire length of stay, but it sets the pattern for the rest of the trip. It is hard for a destination to recover from a poorly handled arrival.

Initial Impressions: These take only a couple of seconds to form, yet tourists use them to make judgements about the rest of the stay. Impressions include both people and physical features. Think about the psychological impact that signposting, driveways, car-parks, entrances, landscaping, the exterior of buildings and paint-work, the presence of litter and so on, have on the arriving tourist. Are local features typical to the area emphasized? Are immovable eyesores converted, perhaps with plants, into something more attractive? Are physical features well maintained and free from safety hazards?

In addition the people who meet the tourist on arrival? What impression do they give? Tourists tend to judge things that they can't see or have yet to see, such as kitchen hygiene or bedroom cleanliness, on the initial appearance of one person. Authenticity may also be a factor. For example, tourists visiting English farms indicated that they liked meeting the farmer in his working clothes as it made the farm more real to them.

Welcome and Greeting: The welcome can help to settle and relax the tourist, plus establish a relationship between the host and tourist that can be most useful in solving any potential complaints before they become an issue. Each culture has its own way of greeting, and this should be designed into the tourism product as it is part of the identity of the destination (see the practical tips below).

PRACTICAL TIPS FOR WELCOMING TOURISTS
✓ What behaviours constitute a typical greeting in the host culture? How do greetings vary by age/relationship/gender?
✓ Always make the first move to greet the tourist; don't wait for them. They may feel unsure of themselves.
✓ Be sensitive to any differences that may exist between the tourist culture and the host culture, in particular with respect to physical space, touch and name use.
✓ If offering something is typical, incorporate it into the greeting. It may be tea, coffee, a glass of local drink, a type of food, or a symbolic good.
✓ Use conversation as appropriate to find out names and to create a rapport that encourages the tourist to speak to you directly should something be unsatisfactory.
✓ Learn a few basic words of greeting in the language of your key foreign tourist segments. Remember that most of the message of welcome that you communicate comes from the way you use your voice and body language. Even if a tourist doesn't understand the words used, she knows whether she is welcome or not.

Queuing, Line-ups and Order: Sometimes the experience involves queuing or some form of order on arrival, and this should be made as pleasant as possible. Insights into queue management are given by Maister (1985). The work shows that:

♦ unoccupied time feels longer to the tourist than occupied time;
♦ post-process waits feel longer than pre-process waits, which feel longer than in-process waits.

The wait should be designed as part of the overall process. If pre-process waits are incorporated by using relevant activities, tourists feel that the experience has already started. As solo waits appear longer than group waits, queue layout can be designed to facilitate conversation, which also occupies time. Maister (1985) also shows that:

- anxiety makes waits appear longer to the tourist;
- uncertain waits appear longer to the tourist than known waits;
- unexplained waits appear longer to the tourist than those that are explained.

These points highlight the importance of information provision and communication with the tourist. Fairness and equity in waits should also be observed. Systems based on the guideline of 'first in first out' can help, for example, a 'take-a-number' type system. The 'multi-line multi-server' queue design does not always promote a sense of justice in waiting as, invariably, one line is seen to move more rapidly than the others.

The Stay Stage

The visit itself is the most obvious stage of the tourist stay and it incorporates many issues and topics. Many of these issues will have been addressed by the destination prior to the arrival of tourists, for example, training programmes or the implementation of complaint management systems. Broadly, the issues can be divided into physical feature issues (getting the product right and information provision), people issues and process issues (complaint management systems). Each issue is examined in turn.

Getting the Product Right: This section refers to separate components of the destination product, for example, accommodation units, attractions or tourist information centres. The physical detail relays messages about product quality. The physical detail can directly influence the emotions, physical comfort and behaviour of the tourist. In addition, contact staff, non-contact staff and residents can also be affected. In developing the product, objectives should be set with regard to desired feelings and behaviour in participants. Such objectives may vary room by room for accommodation. Possible ideas for emotional objectives include creating feelings of warmth and welcome (the hallway), encouraging relaxation and restfulness (the bedroom), engendering calmness (airport facilities) or excitement (white-knuckle theme parks), formality (large dining-room), grandeur (heritage property) or inspiration (place associated with a famous personality).

Possible ideas for behavioural objectives include prompting the tourist to carry out certain tasks, facilitating mixing and sociability, increasing spend per head, increasing or decreasing length of time spent, or controlling the direction of flow or volume of movement. Consider McDonald's as a standardized, globally recognizable example. The hard, shiny surfaces, fixed seating, hard chairs, big glass windows, bright lighting, bold colours, oversized writing, spatial layout and signage are all designed to lure people in, encourage them to spend and to participate as required in the process (clearing away trays, fetching condiments etc.) and not to linger. McDonald's want a fast turnaround. Compare these objectives to those of a cosy restaurant and contrast the use of the physical detail. Table 8.3 provides a checklist of physical detail to help achieve particular objectives. Again, authenticity can be used to create a sense of place or identity.

Checklist	Comment
• Lighting	Natural, low, bright, coloured, energy-saving ...
• Sound	Music, water, volume, repetition ...
• Temperature/humidity	Ventilation, heating, air-conditioning ...
• Colour/patterns	Emotion, warm, cool, hue, brightness, matt, contrast ...
• Texture	Hard, soft, contrast, rough, smooth ...
• Size and shape	Angular, rounded, large, small, miniature, oversized ...
• Layout	Space, texture of walking surfaces, signage, functionality, process facilitation, flexibility ...
• Printed material	Folders, leaflets, compliment slips, paper, texture, print, logo ...
• Clothes	Uniforms, professional, maintenance, reflection of lifestyle/product ...
• Smell	Cooking smells, cleanliness, fresh, disguise unpleasant odours ...
• Security/privacy	Outside lighting, textured glass, locks on doors & windows, fire escapes ...
• Health	Ease of cleaning surfaces, first-aid box, allergies, pillows, plants & animals ...
• Authenticity	Local styles and materials, man-made, natural, fabrics, pottery, local crafts, lace and embroidery, rugs, tablecloths, bowls of locally grown fruit ...

Table 8.3: Checklist for Physical Detail

Information Provision: Although tourists will have received information prior to their arrival, groups vary in their ability or interest in absorbing facts. Once at the destination, carefully designed information can:

♦ equip tourists for day-to-day living. For example, the nearest petrol station, dry cleaners, chemist, post office, tourist information centre, bus and train stations, taxi and car hire. Details should include opening days and times, contact numbers and prices.

♦ reassure tourists for emergency services. For example, the local police, doctor, nurse, hospital, or fire station.

♦ give guidelines for appropriate behaviour and any explanations for such guidelines.

♦ encourage tourists to spend money locally in a range of places. For example, bars, shops, restaurants, clubs, craft and souvenir outlets.

♦ persuade tourists to increase their length of stay or to return for a second visit. For example, providing information on primary attractions and activities, excursions, circular routes, lesser-known attractions and activities, festivals and events at different times of the year.

♦ increase tourist understanding of the destination through interpretation of customs, myths, landmarks, notable characters and so forth.

Information can be collated in a loose-leaf file allowing for the regular updating of material. Leaflets of attractions and activities can be included. Libraries of books and pamphlets on local history, flora and fauna, novels by local authors and so on can also promote relaxation in rooms where this is desirable. Language books and phrase books might be included. Some destinations produce small leaflets or cards translating key phrases of use to tourists into the local language.

Written information is standardized, whereas the knowledge of contact staff allows a colourful and customized approach to imparting local information that some tourist segments are eager to tap into. Setting time aside to help with itineraries or to answer specific questions can greatly enhance the tourist experience. Some tourists prefer to feel that they have 'discovered' a craft shop or small bistro for themselves; hosts should be sensitive to this need for exploration.

With regard to buying non-essential goods, tourists will spend either if the items are cheaper than they are at home (branded goods) or if the items are different (handmade crafts typical to the locality). Destinations must draw a clear distinction between genuine handicrafts based on traditional skills that can command a premium price and souvenir items that resemble local crafts but are mass produced. Tourists must be confident in what they are purchasing; rip-offs damage repeat and referred business. Destinations may want to explore ways of protecting traditional skills and trade marks and communicating these to the tourist.

Some nationalities and cultures favour souvenir items, because the giving of small presents to many acquaintances is expected of them upon their return. Leisure shopping is a classic tourist activity whose importance in terms of temporal and monetary spend is underestimated in survey research. Given the opportunity, certain tourist segments tend to spend more time and money on shopping than they are comfortable admitting to.

Finally, it is briefly noted that facilitating tourists to buy local crafts, drinks and food produce not only spreads the tourist spend in the immediate locality with beneficial knock-on effects, but can also help to stimulate export of these goods to foreign countries, thus helping the agricultural and manufacturing industries. Tourism can provide a showcase for such potential exports.

People Skills: It is said that a prerequisite to long-term tourist satisfaction is staff satisfaction. Unhappy staff and residents cannot produce happy tourists. This is not always properly recognized by the tourism industry, which is characterized by its relatively low pay, high job seasonality and high staff turnover. Notwithstanding, there is a strong emphasis on human resource management, in particular, recruitment processes, training, motivation, appraisal and reward systems. For example, reward systems should support both the hard and soft standards set in the quality system. Too often, reward systems focus on the hard aspects at the expense of the soft, less-readily quantifiable elements.

The work by Parasuraman et al. (1988) suggests that organizations should develop three dimensions (alongside reliability and physical clues) that tourists use to assess service quality. These three dimensions are suited to the setting of soft standards:

♦ responsiveness of staff, or the willingness of staff to help tourists promptly;

♦ assurance of staff, or the knowledge and courtesy of staff and their capacity to invoke trust and confidence;

♦ empathy of staff, or the ability of staff to offer tourists caring and individual attention.

Destinations should also think in terms of recruiting, training and rewarding other participants. Tourists are 'recruited' through the process of segmentation (see Chapter 5), and should be 'trained' in appropriate behaviours and to understand their role in any service process. Non-contact staff provide support services to contact staff, and this chain is only as strong as the weakest link. Destinations can create community lists of recommended suppliers, such as plumbers, farmers, craftsmen, computer engineers, office equipment etc., from locally based businesses. This helps to integrate tourism into other local industry sectors, tightening links, and circulating more of the tourist spend around the local economy. Some destinations run 'adopt a farmer' schemes for hotels to strengthen and diversify local agriculture and to decrease any reliance on imported foodstuffs.

Training for staff should be ongoing, and can be a mix of formal and informal techniques (see the practical tips below). Teamwork and task flexibility to cope with variations in demand should be encouraged. Some organizations adopt a policy of staff empowerment, or of pushing the authority and responsibility for decision-making from managers to contact staff. Empowerment requires training for managers and staff alike.

PRACTICAL TIPS FOR TRAINING
✓ Existing courses by national tourist boards or training boards, including distance learning.
✓ Topics covering food and hygiene, legislative requirements, first aid, languages, marketing, customer care and brochure production.
✓ Guest speakers at local meetings, such as police on improving security, fire officers, insurance representatives, national tourist board officers, environmental health officers, tourist information centre supervisors, etc.
✓ Hold meetings in accommodation units and rotate venues so that people gain inspiration for product improvements. Drives up standards through friendly rivalry.
✓ If grading and classification-type schemes operate, hold a mock inspection as a training vehicle.
✓ Group trips to other destinations can help prevent an inward-product focus, stimulate new ideas and be motivating for participants.
✓ Role play can help develop conversation, listening and complaint handling skills.

Complaint Management Systems: Complaints are usually seen as a bad thing for any destination, but this is not necessarily true. Complaints:

♦ give the destination important information about product performance and tourist satisfaction;

♦ offer the destination an opportunity to take corrective action and recover the situation.

A dissatisfied tourist will relay his bad experience to about 20 other people, while a satisfied tourist tells around five people. Thus, negative word of mouth spreads faster than positive word of mouth (the backbone of referred business). Moreover, for every one complaint received, there are certain to be other tourists with the same complaint who do not bring it to the attention of the destination. Yet they still spread the word to friends and acquaintances. If complaints are caught early enough and resolved, a dissatisfied tourist can be converted into a satisfied one.

Complaints must not be treated on an *ad hoc* basis, but as part of a system (see Figure 8.6, page 179). If complaints are encouraged, then they can be dealt with as they occur and before they become serious problems fuelled by frustration. Establishing a rapport through the initial welcome and engaging in informal conversation can be useful techniques for identifying a complaint in its infancy. Staff should be trained and empowered to handle complaints themselves, rather than referring all cases to management. Practical tips are given as a list of 'do's' and 'don'ts' to help staff better handle complaints (see the *Practical Tips*, page 178). Of course, once a complaint has become a letter or formal complaint, then a different process is needed. Hard standards should be set for response times to such letters.

The Departure Stage

Destinations sometimes forget to manage the last impression that the tourist has on departure. Attention should be paid to the physical clues and to the personal contact. For example, how attractive is the exit? The coach or rail station? The petrol garage? How friendly are the staff?

As for the welcome, farewells should reflect the host culture. Is a small gift appropriate? Drink or food for the journey? Some hosts give a postcard of their establishment with their name and address printed on the back. Some of the practical tips for welcoming tourists are equally relevant for the farewell. The last impression of a destination must be favourable.

The Memories Stage

Stories are told, photographs passed round, videos played and souvenirs admired. This is the stage where positive word-of-mouth recommendation is implemented, helping to create referred business. Perceived as unbiased, the advice of a tourist familiar with the destination is sought and a satisfied tourist can become a valued advocate for the destination.

PRACTICAL TIPS FOR STAFF HANDLING COMPLAINTS

✓ **DO** dress professionally as this sends positive signals

✓ **DO** remain calm and confident

✗ **DON'T** argue with the tourist

✓ **DO** use positive body language

✓ **DO** establish and maintain eye contact

✗ **DON'T** raise your voice or shout

✓ **DO** observe and listen carefully – allow the tourist to speak

✓ **DO** apologize that the situation has happened and thank the tourist for raising the matter with you

✗ **DON'T** blame colleagues in front of the tourist

✓ **DO** take responsibility for solving the problem

✓ **DO** ask questions to find out more information

✗ **DON'T** be aggressive

✓ **DO** summarize information to check mutual understanding

✓ **DO** analyse the information regarding cause and behaviour

✗ **DON'T** personalize the situation

✓ **DO** present alternative solutions, any explanations and then agree on a solution

✓ **DO** carry out the agreed solution or check that it is carried out

✗ **DON'T** offer excuses

✓ **DO** check that the tourist is satisfied with the final outcome

✗ **DON'T** reach conclusions before you have sufficient information

IN SOME INSTANCES:

✓ **DO** walk and talk to the tourist at the same time maintaining eye contact – useful for removing the complainer from a public area

✓ **DO** refer the problem to management if necessary or the tourist insists

✓ **DO** take notes on incidents as a precautionary measure immediately afterwards

✓ **DO** coax the tourist to tell you about a problem if you think they are reluctant to speak to you

WHAT NEXT?

This chapter has discussed issues surrounding customer satisfaction and customer care. Along with previous chapters on marketing and planning, success in customer care relies on relevant and timely information drawn from research to reduce the risk in the decisions taken and to monitor progress made. It is the crucial process of research that will be examined in Chapter 9.

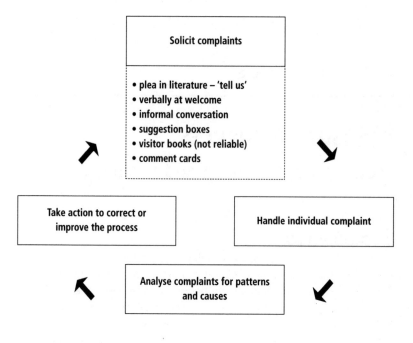

Figure 8.6: Complaint Management Systems

FURTHER READING *on Keeping the Tourist*
Zeithaml, V.A. and Bitner, M.J. (1996) *Services Marketing*. London: McGraw-Hill.

CHAPTER NINE

Measuring success
Monitoring, research and evaluation

INTRODUCTION

A critical element of any tourism development strategy is to measure what has been achieved set against what it was designed to do in the first place. Tourism destination development begins with an assessment of local resources and visitor markets, but does not simply end with plan implementation. To do so would leave the plan indefensible in terms of meeting its goals and objectives. It is therefore essential that before development takes place, or is further encouraged, a system to monitor and evaluate the effectiveness of such actions is set in place. After all, if you don't know where you've started from, you can't really say if you've been successful or not.

Monitoring and evaluation are also important for knowing what is happening with tourism in a destination; an essential element in managing its impacts. Monitoring helps to identify problems before they get out of hand, to adapt to a changing marketplace, as well as measure the response to specific initiatives. However, if this is to be effective, monitoring and evaluation needs to take place on a regular and systematic basis, involving economic, social and environmental indicators of both supply and demand:

♦ **In terms of supply** – monitoring typically involves the assessment of occupancy levels, attendance figures and transportation flows against predevelopment values. It also means assessing the response of the destination's resident community to development and the effects tourism has had on local quality of life;

♦ **In terms of demand** – monitoring usually means collecting data on visitor satisfaction, market origins and travel motivations to help

better focus activities and guide future revision of the
development plan itself. It also helps to determine how effective
the strategy has been in terms of matching supply with demand.

With this in mind, this chapter looks at a number of methods commonly
applied to the measurement and review of tourism development and marketing activity. The discussion which follows is meant to provide a general
introduction to these techniques, where they are more commonly applied,
and some indication of their relative strengths and limitations, both in
terms of reliability and ease of use. It is not meant as a definitive or comprehensive review and readers who require a more detailed explanation,
or seek a more in-depth discussion of their relative merits and application,
are referred to the texts listed at the end of this chapter.

TECHNIQUES FOR MONITORING PERFORMANCE
Tourism monitoring can be accomplished in several ways, using a variety of
techniques and methods. Broadly speaking these fall into two categories:
qualitative (understanding issues in depth) and *quantitative* (the statistical
analysis of numerical data). Qualitative techniques tend to collect detailed
information from small representative groups, where the aim of the
research is to develop an understanding of an issue or to look for meaning
in personal attitudes and prejudice. They are not meant to describe or
measure large group thinking, but can provide the basis for developing a
more quantitative study later on. By comparison, quantitative techniques
are based on the analysis of numbers: visitor numbers, ticket sales, satisfaction levels, etc. Neither approach is necessarily better than the other, but
rather some techniques are more appropriate or useful depending on the
circumstance of application. Indeed, sometimes one technique feeds off the
other and vice versa.

However, for some aspects of tourism monitoring, data may already be
available, having been collected by other organizations such as a regional
or national tourist board, individual visitor attractions and facilities, or
other sections of the industry, such as transport, catering and accommodation providers. This type of *secondary data* is often very useful in developing a broader picture of tourist activity, which can help supplement
primary data sources, and act as an additional point for comparison. It is
generally worthwhile looking at secondary sources because of this, but
also because it can help to identify gaps in current levels of information, is
relatively cheap to use compared to new data collection, and similarly as
they already exist, save both time and effort. However, for many local

destinations, secondary sources are not always readily available. This section now looks briefly at secondary sources before a more in-depth look at the application of both qualitative and quantitative techniques in tourism monitoring and research.

Secondary Data Sources

Information is the foundation of good decision-making. In many destination regions and countries, tourism boards and other government agencies, or indeed the private sector, routinely collect statistical information on tourist travel patterns, origins, socio-demographic variables and their activities. These types of surveys provide valuable information on regional trends and activity, both seasonally and over the longer term. They can be very useful for identifying the general character of tourism activity in proximity to a destination, and give some indication of the size and structure of the existing tourism marketplace.

Secondary data sources which can be applied to tourism monitoring come in all shapes and sizes, ranging from national exit surveys at international air- and seaports, to, for example, the published attendance figures from the neighbouring community's annual summer festival. Some of this information may be very detailed and readily available for anyone to see, while other sources may be commercially sensitive or confidential with only aggregate or gross figures released. Other relevant sources include general economic, retail spending, leisure activity and census surveys undertaken by many national governments or their agencies. These surveys provide data on domestic spending habits, travel patterns, leisure activities and socio-economic characteristics of the population which can then be examined in the context of the destination's current visitor market.

However, while secondary data has its obvious benefits to the destination, information relating to regional or national tourism patterns, or to leisure preference and activity can be very pernicious for individual destinations if not read with caution. For example:

♦ **travel patterns** – at the national level, international tourism may be quite significant to the country as a whole, but this does not mean all individual destinations or even regions within that country will necessarily attract any foreign visitors. Similarly, two destination communities in close proximity may share political, geographical or socio-cultural similarities, but this does not mean they will attract exactly the same type of visitor, either domestic or foreign.

♦ **leisure preference** – survey respondents tend to exaggerate their performance or preference for different types of activities. What people say they do, or would like to do does not necessarily reflect reality. For example, while a national survey of leisure interests may show that some population groups would like to try bungee-jumping, white-water rafting, or scuba-diving for their potential excitement, whether or not these people will actually pursue the activity is uncertain.

Thus, while secondary data may help paint a broader picture of tourism and leisure activity, how this will be relevant to each destination must be carefully examined in each situation. Making decisions based solely on secondary data sources can be dangerous, as it could lead to policy and development plans that do not adequately reflect the local situation and, hence, should be avoided. This does not mean that secondary sources should be avoided altogether, but rather should be used in concert with qualitative and quantitative studies with a direct relationship to the destination in question.

QUALITATIVE ANALYSIS

Qualitative analysis is very useful in developing a more detailed understanding of a particular issue, as opposed to simply measuring it. In tourism planning and marketing these issues include the understanding of tourist (or resident) attitudes, beliefs, feelings and images for a given destination. It may also include generating new ideas for development, testing reaction to creative promotional concepts or new products, or perhaps exploring a particular problem prior to establishing survey research. Qualitative methods are particularly useful for tourism analysis because they can help us better to understand the tourist experience from a personal point of view and explore issues more in-depth.

There are a number of different techniques or methods used in qualitative analysis. However, this chapter will limit its discussion to what may be considered the more classic techniques of qualitative analysis: *focus groups*, *personal interviews*, *observation* and *projective techniques*. The following sections look at each of these methods in terms of their practical application and execution.

Focus Groups

A focus group is a discussion session led by a moderator convened to explore a particular topic in an unstructured or semi-structured manner. For best results with group dynamics, no fewer than six and no more than ten respondents should be used in any one session. It is, however, wise to run two to four separate focus groups (with different respondents), rather than to rely on the results from a solitary group.

Objectives: The objectives for focus group research should address what you want to find out, but set in a broad context. Objectives are often exploratory in nature.

Recruiting Respondents: The researcher needs to consider the respondent make-up of the group. Is a homogeneous group that mirrors a certain tourist segment required, or a mix of respondents with its inherent conflicts? Is a probability or non-probability sampling technique preferable? Often a convenience sample or quota sample is used, with a brief questionnaire to screen potential respondents for relevant characteristics. For a destination, it is easiest to capture respondents during the stay, rather than before or after, but this creates problems by disrupting the holiday mood. It may help to provide leisure-based incentives that will enhance the rest of the trip, for example, reduced entry fees to attractions. Alternatively, certain tourists can be intercepted at the airport (preferably by prior arrangement), although available time will be a limiting factor and tensions may be running high. It is also important to remember that vacation decisions are taken in a social context and rarely by a single individual. Due consideration should be given to *influencers*, *deciders*, *information gatherers* and *purchasers*, as well as the actual users, in focus group formation.

Designing the Setting: The location should offer a room with an informal atmosphere and the organizer should consider the physical comfort of respondents. Think about using the hospitality rooms at a local hotel or tourist attraction. Soft drinks should be provided and easy chairs for relaxation. As the tourism experience is one associated with leisure rather than work (the exception being business tourism which spans the two), the atmosphere should provide a continuation of the enjoyment. For respondents, the discussion group should not remind them of work. Recording devices, whether videotape or audiocassette, should be as out of sight as possible and certainly not referred to during the session.

Running the Session: Each session should be between one and two hours long. This gives the moderator time to establish rapport with the group and to delve deeply into the designated issues. The skills of the facilitator drive the success of the group. Aspects of what makes a good moderator can be gleaned from the points below on running a session. Many of the skills are used in everyday communication, but they are often forgotten by poor moderators who talk too much or fail to remain neutral.

✓ The moderator should introduce themselves to each individual as they arrive.

✓ Each respondent should be invited to introduce themselves to the others at the beginning of the session.

✓ The moderator should give a short introduction to the session and introduce the rules. These may include affirming that there are no right or wrong opinions, just opinions; one person to talk at any one time; the need to hear from everyone; no questions to the moderator as their opinions are unimportant, and so on. The moderator should answer any questions concerning how the session will run.

✓ The moderator should encourage everyone to speak in the first five minutes as this reduces stress in individuals early on and will encourage them to contribute later.

✓ Keep the questions simple and ask only one at a time. Questions are posed to generate discussion, so open questions requiring development in the answer are preferable to those demanding a 'yes' or 'no' response.

✓ Silence is not a problem, so moderators should be wary of breaking in with another question. Allow respondents time to reflect.

✓ Treat all respondents with equal respect. Try referring back to previous ideas or comments and using the respondent's name; both show moderator responsiveness.

✓ Ensure that a few respondents don't dominate the group, squeezing out those more reluctant to speak. Body language can draw out the shy and shut down the talkative; smiles, forward body language and continuous eye contact bring a speaker on,

contd

---

whereas withdrawal can quieten those inclined to dominate. In addition, by saying 'that's an interesting point; I'd like to see how everyone else feels about that', the shy can be coaxed forwards while the dominating can be constrained.

✓ Observe the variations in energy levels in the group and the body language used; this is as relevant to communication as the words spoken.

✓ Don't rely on the spoken word; words can be constraining and the introduction of other techniques can enliven a discussion group. Projective techniques might play a role (see Projective Techniques, page 189) and stimulus material can also be useful. This may involve group tasks such as cutting and pasting pictures from magazines in a montage to reflect the image of the destination, or discussion around competitors' brochures or other visible objects such as holiday snaps, or preprepared image boards.

✓ When a respondent makes a controversial statement, the role of the moderator is to legitimize that opinion before others try to put it down, for example by saying 'an interesting point; I've heard others say that in sessions'.

✓ The moderator should signal that the end of the session is approaching at least five minutes before it closes. This creates the time for any final remarks to be made, any corrections, and the group to round itself off rather than being cut mid-flow.

✓ The moderator should always thank the respondents for giving up their valuable time to participate in the group.

Analysis: Audiocassettes and videotapes are best transcribed (with additional comment on body language where applicable) prior to analysis. Responses should be related back to objectives. The researcher should look for areas of general consensus, depth of feeling, any differences between separate focus groups (or where the group itself was mixed) and responses that challenge assumptions. It is a selective process, with superficial data being discarded and a coding system may be required.

The analyst should be wary of taking responses at face value. The meaning behind the words gives the most valuable information. For instance:

- 'Its quite nice I guess' [Awful! I hate it!]

- 'It would be OK for backpackers' [Its cheap and shoddy ... fine for them]

- 'Some people might like that brochure front cover' [But not me; I wouldn't pick it up]

The responses should be interpreted and their possible relevance to any decisions to be taken explained. Reporting the facts lifted from the focus groups is not sufficient.

Personal Interviews

Much of the practical detail given under focus groups can be adapted for personal interviews. Obviously, highly structured one-to-one interviews are a method of survey research. Here, we are concerned with qualitative interviews. Broadly speaking, there are two types:

- *semi-structured personal interviews* with a respondent where the interviewer directs the line of questioning from a preprepared interview schedule. Topics can be developed and the order changed, because the research design is very flexible, yet the interviewer has pre-decided the areas of relevance. Typical duration is around 30 to 45 minutes.

- *unstructured personal interviews* with an informant where the interviewer has no prepared schedule but is directed by the informant. Typical duration is one to two hours, and a series of interviews may be held with the same informant.

Tourism management often uses the semi-structured approach to interviewing. Generally, individual interviews are preferable to focus groups where individuals are subject to peer pressure or where the information is either sensitive or complex. Organizers should consider the following points:

♦ appropriate sampling technique and number of respondents required (remember, the aim is to understand, not to measure, so small samples are justifiable). Snowballing may be useful where a number of experts are needed; after each interview, the expert is asked to suggest a further expert in the area to be contacted by the interviewer.

♦ data can be recorded by taking notes or by using an audiocassette. The latter is better unless the information is considered sensitive by the respondent or where a recorder's presence may inhibit the development of the conversation. Tape recording requires prior consent from the respondent.

♦ additional sources of evidence, such as brochures, documents, advertisements and so on, may provide support for findings or act as a cross-reference point.

♦ questions should start with those designed to relax the respondent, and then work from the general to the specific in a 'funnel' effect. Probing can add examples or extra detail.

♦ thought must be given to the training of field interviewers where a team is used. Consistency in probing is important.

♦ interviewers need to remain neutral and non-judgmental and to empathize with the respondent. Accent, dress, facial expressions, voice and so on can all influence the performance of the interviewer.

♦ data should be treated as confidential and an individual should only be identified in a report by a code number.

Observation Techniques

Everybody makes casual observation, often relayed as anecdotes. Observation as a research technique raises it from the casual to the planned. In tourism, with its advantages of having the consumer on-site, it is a surprisingly neglected research tool. According to Tull and Hawkins (1993), the data must be observable (for example, a certain type of behaviour, a physical action, verbal action, facial expression, temporal pattern, or related to spatial use), must happen frequently, repetitively and predictably, and must only occupy a short time span. Observation can also be divided into:

♦ *natural vs. contrived* – tourism is suited to a natural setting, although a laboratory may be used in certain circumstances.

♦ *open vs. disguised* – the observer may be disguised as a fellow visitor, or concealed behind a one-way mirror, or may be openly seen by the tourist. The first raises ethical issues of disguise, while the second raises issues of observer influence in the selected behaviour. Mystery shopping to check the quality of competitors makes use of disguised observation.

♦ *direct vs. indirect* – with tourism happening at the destination, it is possible to observe tourist activity in real time. However, indirect methods may be appropriate, such as measuring the wear and tear of carpets to identify popular exhibits, or dustbin audits to check eating and drinking habits.

♦ *human vs. mechanical* – human observers can mingle well amongst tourists, but some situations may require mechanical methods. Video cameras, closed-circuit television, or time-lapse photography can be useful.

As the observation is planned, a structured observation sheet may be relevant for human observation. This sheet should record the date, time, location, observer name and weather (as appropriate), before itemizing those actions to be observed. A stopwatch may be needed to measure lengths of time for actions, such as queuing. The basic data analysis will establish the sequence and patterns of actions and frequency counts before taking the analysis further.

Projective Techniques

These may form part of a focus group or personal interview. They may be defined as covert or hidden/disguised techniques that are unstructured and indirect and that allow the respondent to project their own beliefs, attitudes or feelings on to a third person or object. They are useful for getting information that the respondent may be unable to express or even be unaware of. Some are suitable for use with younger visitors. Projective techniques are based on ambiguous stimuli. Rooted in clinical psychology, analysis can be complex, but used at a simple level, they can nonetheless offer insights into feelings, images or stereotypes for tourism managers.

Some of the projective techniques most applicable for destination research include:

♦ *Word association* – where the respondent is asked to say the first word that comes to mind. The list of stimulus words should include neutral words, random words and the test words (brand names, competitors, names of places, etc.). The list should be read out by the interviewer; spontaneity of answer is crucial. Basic analysis should include the frequency of response words, hesitation and non-response.

♦ *Sentence or story completion* – where the respondent is asked to finish off a sentence or story about a third character. Responses should be checked at face value and interpreted at the deeper level.

♦ *Personification* – where the respondent is asked to describe the destination (or competitor etc.) as something else, for example, as an animal or as a person. Some organizations have asked respondents to write obituaries for their products or brands.

♦ *Consumer drawings* – where the respondent is asked to draw a typical tourist visiting destination 'x', or visitor using attraction 'y'.

♦ *Cartoon tests* – where the respondent is shown a cartoon and is asked to fill in the speech bubbles of the characters. Some cartoons contain thought bubbles as well, which allow the hidden meaning behind the words to be expressed.

♦ *Picture response* – where respondents are shown a picture and are asked to describe, for example, what happened before, next, the feelings of the characters and so on.

♦ *Third-person tests* – where the respondent projects their attitudes on to a vague third person under the guise of 'most tourists' or 'most residents'. One version is to present two identical lists of purchases to two different groups and ask them to describe the purchaser. Only one item in the list is different and it is this item to which any differences in opinion may be attributed. For example, the odd one out amongst a list of purchased or used services may be a two-day break at destination x.

♦ *Play techniques* – where respondents are asked to sort, rank or group objects, cards or words, perhaps first spontaneously according to their own feelings and then by direction. For example, a list of destinations may be generated and then sorted by the type of visitor.

Although projective techniques should not be overrelied upon in tourism research when used by non-psychologists, they can be good at stimulating fresh thought, uncovering a new angle, or simply enlivening a focus group or interview.

QUANTITATIVE TECHNIQUES

Quantitative methods are different from those used in qualitative research primarily due to their focus on statistical analysis. They also tend to be the more commonly applied methods of tourism analysis because, in principle, they are easier to understand and execute, but also because of the seemingly insatiable appetite of both government and business to have reams and reams of data to help support policy actions and activity. As a result, much of what is frequently (although not accurately) considered as the quantitative approach concerns the development and operation of survey research, and in particular, questionnaire surveys.

While there are other quantitative techniques such as 'research panels', 'opinion polls' and 'Delphi studies' which can be applied to the monitoring of tourism development, this section will focus its discussion on the issues and application of questionnaire-based surveys.

Questionnaire Surveys

Questionnaire-based survey research is (in theory) very simple in the sense that it basically involves asking a lot of people the same set of questions, and then examining their response in terms of straightforward counts or 'frequencies' (descriptive or nominal analysis), or comparisons (correlation) between different groups of respondents (ordinal analysis), or both. However, despite this apparent simplicity, the questionnaire survey can be a fairly complicated analytical tool, and if not carefully planned, the results could easily lead a destination to take decisions based on findings which are not justified. Far too often when presented with statistics, people believe they are reading research results of a certain accuracy, just because they are written down and expressed in numerical form. Sadly this is not always the case, and the root of this error is found in the issue of bias, due to mistakes made in the survey design and execution.

Survey bias (or error) becomes a part of survey research due to a number of different reasons, including *questionnaire delivery* (postal, site, group, etc.) which in turn relates to *sample size and selection, question type* and *design*, and overall levels of *data confidence*:

Questionnaire Delivery: Survey data is collected using what is termed a survey schedule, more commonly referred to as a questionnaire. Generally, these can be completed in one of two ways:

♦ *self-completion* – where the respondent is given a copy of the questionnaire and fills it out on their own, without reference to whomever is conducting the research. They may be handed out and collected on-site, or handed out but returned via the post;

♦ *interviewer completed* – where the interviewer asks people questions, based on the questionnaire, but fills in the response themselves. The interviewers are not meant to interpret the question but simply to read out questions and record the response.

Whether a questionnaire is self-completion or based on the interviewer depends on the actual type of survey schedule in use. In tourism analysis, the three most common types of questionnaire are *street-*, *site-* and *postal-based* surveys:

♦ *street surveys* are, as the name suggests, questionnaires which are distributed in public places, most often on the street in main tourist areas, and/or shopping precincts which tourists tend to patronize in a destination. The questionnaire format is predominately (although not always) completed by the research team by stopping visitors and asking them a number of quick questions (quick being the operative word, as tourists are there to see the destination, not stand around and answer questions). Five minutes is considered the maximum time that should be planned for recording tourist answers. This time frame clearly limits the number of questions and hence the quantity of information which can be collected using this format.

♦ **site surveys** are similar to street surveys, but are generally designed to collect information from users of particular facilities or attractions. Either self- or interviewer-based, this form of survey research is very common in the private sector, where attraction managers, hoteliers, airlines and others use the opportunity to distribute questionnaires to their respective customers. Site surveys have the advantage over street surveys in that they are seen by respondents to be more directly linked to visitor activity and hence tend to be more willing to participate than if just stopped in the street. This also means the questionnaire can be a bit longer (up to 10 minutes to complete), which lends itself to the collection of more detailed or wider points of information.

♦ **postal surveys** are returned to the research team (and occasionally distributed) via the postal service. The postal survey is very common in tourism research, because it allows for a wide distribution of questionnaires and is relatively cheap to operate. However, it also suffers from the highest level of non-response (or low completion rates) compared to the numbers sent out or distributed. They are by their nature self-completion questionnaires which do not have the same time restrictions so evident in street and site surveys. However, if they appear too long (i.e. more than two or three sides of paper), then the same time principle applies with people reluctant to take the time to fill in a lengthy questionnaire and put it in the post.

Each of these methods, whether self-completion or otherwise, have both strengths and drawbacks. The self-completion methods tend to be cheaper because they are not as labour intensive (in terms of actual data collection), compared to interviewer-based completions. However, self-completion questionnaires are notorious for their low response rates and gaps in the level of completion, whereas interviewer completions tend to mean a fuller and more accurate response. In either case, and with each format of delivery, these problems reflect another source of error: sample size and participant selection.

Sample Size and Selection: Questionnaire surveys tend to involve large numbers of people (those answering the questions) ranging from a couple of hundred to a few thousand, clearly depending on the destination and its markets. However, tourism surveys are not meant to question every last visitor, every user of the attraction, or every person going into the tourist information centre. The costs of doing so would prove prohibitive in most situations and in busy periods it would be virtually impossible and a logistical nightmare to ensure every visitor received, completed and returned a questionnaire. For these and other reasons survey research employs a system of *sampling* which seeks to question a smaller but *representative sample* of the destination's total tourist population. However, what is meant by representative and how many this will involve become new points of possible bias or sampling error.

In terms of sample size, generally the larger the total number of respondents (all things being equal) the greater the likelihood of achieving a representative sample. However, this does not mean that in order for the sample to be relatively error free that some minimum number of responses (in relation to the total population) must be achieved. If this were true, virtually all tourism surveys would be at risk, because it is very difficult to be absolutely sure how many visitors any destination actually receives, no matter how meticulous the counting. There may be some very accurate estimates, based on highly structured and methodical counting systems, but generally total tourist populations are only best estimates and sometimes not even best. The basic principle in sampling remains (all things being equal) the larger the sample group, the less likelihood of sampling error.

The key to sample size concerns the issue of *representation*. If the data is collected from a sample which proportionately reflects the wider tourist population, then a sample of 200 is as equally valid as a sample of 2,000 or 20,000. Notwithstanding sample size, however, a truly representative sample means all members of the population (in this case all tourists visiting a destination throughout the year) have an *equal chance* of being selected to participate in the research. Yet the likelihood of this occurring depends very much on the type of questionnaire delivery:

♦ **street surveys** – representative sampling from a street survey is difficult to achieve. A key limitation is that not all tourists in a destination will see the same attractions or go to the same places, and depending on the location of those conducting the research, not everyone will have an equal chance of being selected to participate. Similarly, this could also mean that some types or groups of tourists may end up being over-represented by virtue of their activity and location relative to interviewer locations;

♦ *site surveys* – these tend to offer a better opportunity to collect a representative sample given the likelihood of entry or exit points which funnel tourists past potential interview sites. However, as noted above, not all tourists will visit all sites, so this method will not achieve a totally representative sample for the destination as a whole. This being said, this method clearly is useful within the site in question.

In either case, visitor patterns are not evenly spread throughout the day, month or year. In most destinations, some variation in tourist types will be evident in the data for different times of the day, and days of the week throughout the year, which can be important to development planning and marketing. Therefore in order to be more representative, survey sampling needs to take place at different times of the day, week and year (and even during different types of weather) if it is to offer all visitors (or types of visitors) an equal chance of participation.

One way to help overcome this type of sampling error is to use what is termed *quota sampling*. Interviewers are given quotas of different types of visitors to approach and interview. Quotas may be based on such things as age, sex, occupation, group size and composition, time of day, season or actual dates (i.e. a holiday). Once interviewers have fulfilled their quota for their different groups or market segments, they reject any further respondents from those categories and concentrate on filling the rest of their quota requirements. While this approach does tend to achieve a representative cross-section of the tourist population, its key limitation is that it requires previous knowledge of the make-up of that population in order to derive the appropriate quota proportions.

Another way partially to overcome this point of error requires taking a strategic or *systematic* approach to sampling. Interviewer instructions indicate that, for example, every tenth person passing by should be interviewed, or every subsequent interview should alternate between the sexes. Of course, another problem is that tourists are rarely on their own and the issue then becomes deciding which member of the group should answer the questions. This can partially be overcome by alternating between the sexes with each group or asking the oldest in the group, or the group leader. In this situation, interviewers are given strict instructions for selecting potential respondents:

'As each interview is complete, choose the next person who passes the position. Do not select respondents by any other means. If a *person declines the invitation to participate, select the next person to pass by.'*

or where the visitor is stationary (e.g. a beach) the instructions could read:

'Follow this (x) route and select and stop at every nth group or person to interview. If they decline to participate, move along to the next group.'

The key point is that all tourists should have an equal chance of being selected (within reason) and interviewers should not consciously pick who they choose to stop and interview, other than by the instructions.

♦ ***postal surveys*** – when questionnaires are collected individually (i.e. as a brochure in the TIC, in hotel rooms, etc.), or handed out to visitors for self-completion, the response rates tend to be low. In these situations as little as 20% return rates are not uncommon, which is not necessarily a problem if the sample is still representative, however, this is not always the case. Some people will not complete the questionnaire for any number of reasons including a lack of interest, uncertainty as to whom the survey is aimed at, time, language problems, or they may be put-off by the structure and design of the questionnaire. This is called *non-response bias* and is unavoidable and relevant to all types of surveys, albeit more prevalent to postal and other forms of self-completion questionnaires.

There are, however, a number of ways which can help to reduce levels of non-response bias, including incentives (prize draw entry, product coupons, discount vouchers), postage-paid reply envelopes, how the questions are asked (question type), the format for response, question ordering, and the overall content and layout of the actual questionnaire.

Question Types: Survey research essentially asks questions in one of two ways, either *open* or *closed*. Both formats have arguments for and against their use depending on the type of survey research in question:

♦ ***open-ended questions*** – these require respondents to provide an answer with their own, unprompted ideas. A typical (albeit often unanswered) open question found on most tourism surveys asks 'any other comments?' Depending on the form of questioning, either the interviewer asks the question and waits for a response, or the survey schedule contains a blank space or lines. The advantage of this type of question is that it allows the participant to provide their own response without undue influence, rather than being forced to choose from some pre-ordained list. However, as a disadvantage, open questions are difficult to analyse, especially when response levels are high (on interviewer-based surveys); they are sometimes difficult to record accurately (in face-to-face interviews); they can annoy the respondent who will then throw the survey in the bin; and as is often the case, particularly on self-completion questionnaires, open questions are invariably left blank, or contain answers often irrelevant to the actual question (at least from the point of view of the research team);

♦ *closed questions* – in contrast, pose a question but then offer the respondent a range of answers or options to choose from. The respondent is directed towards a particular type of answer (typically by ticking a box, or circling a number/letter) which the research team believes will address the issue being examined. Closed questions range from the basic 'yes or no' response, to various forms of scales and selection criteria from predetermined lists. The advantages of a closed question are that they are very easy statistically to analyse, they tend to achieve high completion rates and provide a definite structure to the response. The key disadvantage is that they limit the range of response to the pre-specified format.

The type of question used is obviously a matter of judgement, depending on the purpose of the research and the format in which the survey schedule will be presented to the tourist. However, in quantitative surveys (as opposed to qualitative research), the more common and practical question format is the closed response, with answers based on *opposites, checklists, rankings, paired comparisons* and *'Likert'* scales:

♦ *opposites* are basically *'yes or no'*, *'black or white'*, *'in or out'* type questions, indicating the presence or absence of different conditions. They are most often used to determine if a specific condition, such as membership of a club, is true of the respondent (e.g. 'are you currently a member of a golf club?');

♦ **checklists** present a series of options/answers from which to choose. They usually ask the respondent: 'Which of the following best represents your views on ...', or 'Which of the following is the most important to you ...' Sometimes checklists also offer a blank or 'other' category, left 'open' for individuals to add their own response, if none of those suggested appears to reflect their views or opinion. Sometimes an open question is connected with checklists asking respondents to explain their choice;

♦ **rankings**, like *checklists*, provide a number of categories to choose from, but require the respondent to place all the options in some order of preference or importance. When asking people to rank-order a series of options, statistical research has shown that the list should not normally exceed seven options, because most people cannot easily differentiate between more than seven different options at one point in time.

   Ranking questions are superior to simple *checklists*, and *opposites* as they collect information which is considered to be of a higher order. That is while the answers provide ranked preference, they can also be examined like a checklist (by selecting just the top-ranked answer) from each respondent. In contrast, it is not legitimate to suggest rankings from the lower order response as provided by the checklist answer.

♦ **paired comparisons** are similar to ranking questions, but require the respondent to indicate a preference between a pair of options in a list. Each item is paired once with each other item (e.g. *A with B, B with C, and C with A*). The sum of preference for each item is then tabulated to give an overall 'ranked' preference for each item (e.g. *B preferred twice, A preferred once* and *C not preferred*). In using paired-comparisons, the issue of bias is generally avoided because each item is always paired with each other item. The main disadvantage of this approach is that the more individual items to consider, the greater the number of pairs (e.g. 5 items means 10 pairs, 6 items means 15 pairs, and 7 items means 21 pairs) which has clear implications for space on the questionnaire if nothing else;

♦ **'Likert'-type scales** (named after their psychologist inventor) require respondents to indicate some level of preference or agreement with a statement, normally based on a standard polar

MEASURING SUCCESS • **199**

scale (i.e. from *'strongly agree'* to *'strongly disagree'*, or *'very important'* to *'very unimportant'*). These types of questions are frequently used in tourism marketing to assess tourist satisfaction and the importance of different things to different market segments (see Chapter 7).

Some statistical research suggests there should be an *even* number of options (e.g. Strongly Agree, Agree, Disagree, Strongly Disagree) which forces the respondent into a position for or against. Others, however, argue the scale should be *uneven*, offering a *neutral, no opinion*, or *neither agree nor disagree* option from which to choose. Who is right is the subject of debate, but what is certain is that there should be as many 'plus' points as there are 'minus' points. Question scales which state *Very Good, Good, Satisfactory* or *Poor* are automatically biased by offering three 'plus' options, but only one 'minus' category, and should be avoided.

All of these question formats are valid and useful in monitoring, particularly in measuring attitudes towards different aspects of tourism in a destination. Attitudes affect destination choice and these techniques can be used to assess tourist reactions, likes and dislikes, satisfaction levels, and expectations. Equally they can be used to monitor resident reaction and support for different forms of tourism activity in the destination community and its impact on 'local' quality of life. Despite these and other benefits, however, these techniques can also generate further response bias depending on the wording and order of questions as they appear on the survey schedule.

Question Wording and Order: Points of bias are often introduced into survey research simply through the wording of questions, their response categories and the order they appear on the survey schedule. Avoiding these errors can go a long way to reducing problems with analysis and raising the validity of the survey research in question. Errors in response tend to arise when questions and answers are *multipurpose*, use *jargon*, are *ambiguous*, are overly *complicated*, or *lead the response* in a certain direction:

♦ *multipurpose questions* cause problems with survey research because the analysis can never be sure what aspect of the question is related to the answer. Sometimes words may appear together in a question which are commonly used together in everyday speech and terminology, such as *'rest and relaxation'*. In this case, it is generally assumed these are describing essentially the same thing. However, if someone were asked to rate the *'quality of service and hospitality'* in a facility, it would be unclear as to whether they were commenting on the *'quality of service'* or the *'hospitality'*. While clearly these two points are linked, and one is part of the other, this type of multipurpose question should be avoided. In this case, it would be best to state these as two separate points of *'quality of service'* and then *'hospitality'*. However, this leads to the second point of error, the use of jargon;

♦ **jargon** refers to specialized language commonly used with reference to a particular subject. In tourism, 'hospitality' is one such word. Generally, people working in tourism will be familiar with its meaning as offering kindness in welcoming guests or strangers. However, what this means to the person answering the questionnaire could be something a little different. The use of jargon can cloud the analysis, because some words may take on a different meaning, depending on how closely the respondent is allied to the subject. Thus if someone was asked to rate 'local hospitality', they may be thinking of how easy it was to find their way around the destination, how they were greeted in attractions, shops or the TIC, the quality of accommodation and restaurant facilities, or what they thought about the friendliness of the whole destination. In this case a dissatisfied response would not really provide any meaningful data if the object of the survey was to assess which aspects of local tourism could do with improvements. This of course leads on to the third point of error, ambiguity in question wording;

♦ **ambiguity** can arise in survey research, both in the wording of the question, and in the categories for response. In terms of the latter, ambiguity happens when closed questions use response lists with categories which overlap. It is a common mistake in survey research to create such lists, particularly when asking questions on income, age, length of stay, estimated expenditure and other forms of numeric data. A response of '3' (in the 'wrong' column) could technically fit in one of two response categories;

Wrong	Better	Best
<1	<1	<1
1 – 3	1 – 2	1 – 2.9
3 – 5	3 – 4	3 – 4.9
5 – 7	5 – 6	5 – 6.9
7 – 9	7 – 8	7 – 8.9
>9	=> 9	=> 9

When possible, it may be better to leave numeric-based questions as an open-ended response, so actual mean (average) values can be computed. Where this becomes a problem is in face-to-face interviews involving questions of a more personal nature, such as age, income and sometimes estimated expenditure.

The other side of ambiguity occurs in the wording of the question. In addition to the use of jargon, questions which use words and phrases that can have more than one interpretation such as 'do you come here a lot?', or 'how often do you come here?' have a number of interpretations depending on what people think is meant by 'a lot' or 'how often' (i.e. once a week, month or year, etc.). Another cause of ambiguity happens with questions containing double negatives. For example, a question asking people to state their level of agreement or support for a statement such as: 'it is not true that tourism does not create employment', would be better stated as 'tourism creates employment'. The original question is unclear, ambiguous and only complicates the response;

♦ **complication** appears often in relation to ambiguous questions and multipurpose questions as noted above. It is also an issue with the structure and order of the questionnaire, especially in the use of filter questions (the answer to one question determines whether or not the respondent should answer the next in sequence, e.g. 'If yes to Question 6, go to Question 10, otherwise go to Question 7'). Layout is particularly important in this case as a complicated structure can cause confusion and hence errors in the response. Question ordering is also relevant when using more complicated question structures (such as attitude ranking) which can also cause problems and put people off from continuing. In this sense, survey schedules should begin with simple and relevant questions (the survey is about tourism, so ask something about tourism), which may then be followed by more complicated question structures which in turn are followed by questions of a more personal nature;

♦ **_leading questions_** represent another cause of bias in survey research. Leading questions tend to encourage people to answer in a certain way, which either lends support to a particular issue, or where a disagreement with the statement would suggest something illogical. For example, a 'yes or no' response to the following could imply two very different things, not just support or rejection for the question:

'Do you believe the Local Council should continue to promote the development of a successful tourism industry?'

Similarly, open-ended questions which ask people to identify key issues or problems can also be considered leading questions, depending on how they are analysed. If such a question were to reveal that only a minority of respondents identified a problem, one approach would be to say that only a few people said ... 'x' ... was an issue, but as this wasn't a majority, we can ignore it. However, this does not mean there were no issues of concern, or that 'x' was only a minor issue, but rather not every respondent was prepared or able to identify the issue, or did not think of it at that point in time. The fact that a minority did identify an issue, without being prompted to look in any particular direction, could suggest there is a real point of concern.

♦ **_sensitive or personal questions_** such as age, income, marital status, address (better to ask for a post code instead), personal spending are best left to the end of the questionnaire. Some people are easily put off by these types of questions, and if they appear at the beginning they may refuse to continue. However, when at the end, people are less likely to balk at these as they have already completed the rest of the form, and the questions then feel less intrusive.

Writing Better Questions: One way to develop a tourism question-naire is to look at what other people have done in a similar situation. However, while their survey schedule may have some relevant points to consider, this does not mean they should be copied verbatim. The operative word here is 'similar', because no two destinations will be in exactly the same position or face the same set of opportunities and constraints. There may be many similarities, but there will always be key differences which need to be taken into account. After all, if all destinations were the same, why travel?

Far too often in survey research, the first thing people do is begin to write down questions that other people have asked, or they've read on another questionnaire, or they think will be interesting to ask. This is the wrong place to start. The first thing to consider is why the survey is necessary. Those preparing the project need to establish what exactly they need to know, and why this type of information is necessary. Then they can begin to consider how they will get it, and in what form or at what level of detail the information will be necessary (i.e. will age groups be okay, or is there a need for more specific age-related data).

Whatever the case, the inclusion of questions must relate to the original issue, with considerable thought given to how the information will be used. All too often tourism surveys include questions which don't readily help answer the original research question, because they haven't been thought through far enough.

To begin to write better questions:

1. first, establish the nature of the issue;

2. then identify the information needs to address that issue;

3. then think of different questions which may provide that information;

4. then think of possible answers people may give;

5. then think of which format is best to ask the question;

6. then test these questions on other people;

7. then compare the response to point 2 and repeat as necessary;
   and then
8. think about how the data will be analysed, as the final test of bias and error in survey research falls to confidence in the interpretation and analysis of the results, and how these are then presented.

<u>Data Confidence and Interpretation</u>: One final major point of error in survey research happens when the data is analysed, with conclusions drawn which are sometimes not justified by the response received. Clearly this relates to sample size and how well that sample is *representative* of the total tourist population (for the destination in question). However, this also relates to the issue of *data confidence* which is a function of sample size and the level of response recorded for specific questions.

In some tourism research, statistical analysis begins (and often ends) with a basic count or 'frequency' of the response to any given question:

e.g. Option *A* = 10%; Option B = 20%; Option *C* = 30%; Option D = 40%

One conclusion from looking at this data (in isolation) would be to suggest that *Option D* (40%) is the most important category, and if this were related to different tourism development opportunities, this might be the option to pursue. However, whether this is the correct interpretation depends on how representative the survey sample is of the total resident or tourist population. The issue is, how confident are we that the data is representative and the results are accurate? The answer lies in *statistical probability* and the *confidence interval*:

♦ ***statistical probability*** is the way in which the precision of research findings are discussed in quantitative analysis. If the sample is truly representative of the tourist or resident population (i.e. drawn at random, each with an equal chance of being included in the research), then the *probability* of the 40% response or preference for *Option D* being correct is fairly high. In contrast, if the sample is not representative, then the true answer could potentially lie anywhere between 0% and 100%, and it would be incorrect to assume this is actually the most popular option.

In quantitative research, statisticians have shown that when a sample is truly representative of the whole 'population', there is a *certain probability* the true answer actually lies somewhere within a *specified range* of the given answer. In tourism research, 'certain probability' tends to refer to what is called the *95% confidence level*. This means that 95% of the time, it would be safe to say the answer for *Option D* is, 'more or less' 40%, whereas 5% of the time this would be an incorrect assumption. The 'more or less' aspect is then referred to as the *confidence interval*. The 'more or less' exists because the response is from a sample and not the whole population.

* ***confidence intervals*** represent the 'specified range' of values
  which define the level of precision for the answer. That is, the
  confidence interval is the number which must be added to, or
  subtracted from the given answer to give the true range of
  response. Confidence intervals are dependent on the total sample
  size (i.e. total number of responses) and the actual response to
  each question item (i.e. Option C = 30% for vs. Option D = 40% etc.).
  (See Figure 9.1).

95% Confidence Intervals			
Response	sample of 100	sample of 200	sample of 500
Option A = 10%	+/– 6.0	+/–4.0	+/–2.6
Option B = 20%	+/– 8.0	+/–5.8	+/–3.6
Option C = 30%	+/– 9.5	+/–6.6	+/–4.1
Option D = 40%	+/– 10.1	+/–6.9	+/–4.4

Figure 9.1: Confidence Intervals and Sample Size – I

95% Confidence Intervals			
Response	sample of 100	sample of 200	sample of 500
Option A = 10%	4.0–16.0	6.0–14.0	7.4–12.6
Option B = 20%	12.0–28.0	14.2–25.8	16.4–13.6
Option C = 30%	20.5–39.5	23.4–36.6	25.9–34.1
Option D = 40%	29.9–50.1	33.1–46.9	35.6–44.4

Figure 9.2: Confidence Intervals and Sample Size – II

The examples given in Figure 9.1 show that if the survey sample size was 100,
then the *Option D* response (of 40%) has a 95% confidence interval of (+/–)
10.1. This means that 95% of the time the answer probably lies anywhere
between 29.9% and 50.1%. If the sample size were increased to 500 respondents and if the answer was still 40%, then 95% of the time statistical probability suggests the answer actually lies anywhere between 35.6% and 44.4%
(see Figure 9.2). As this brief example suggests, the smaller the sample size,
the larger the confidence interval, and when the sample size falls below 100
the range of the confidence interval becomes so large the statistic effectively

becomes meaningless. (Statistical tables and formulas exist which can be used to calculate confidence intervals for all levels of response and sample size, but the smaller the sample size, the larger the confidence interval becomes.)

How confidence intervals and probability are relevant to survey bias is explained using the 'Development Options' data listed above: (e.g. Option A =10%; Option B = 20%, etc.). If the point of the research is to decide which tourism development option is the most favoured or most appropriate for the destination, at first glance it would seem that Option D with 40% has won. If, however, on closer inspection, the sample size is revealed to be only 200 respondents then (as the data in Figure 9.2 shows), despite the 10% difference between Option D and Option C, the *confidence intervals* actually overlap:

$$\text{Option } C: (30\% +/- 6.6) = 23.4\% \text{ to } 36.6\%$$
$$\text{Option } D: (40\% +/- 6.9) = 33.1\% \text{ to } 46.9\%$$

This means there is no 'significant difference' between these two options, and it would be incorrect to say that Option D was the most favoured development opportunity compared to Option C. However, if this same result was based on a sample size of 500, then the confidence intervals would be smaller and the overlap in categories would not exist:

$$\text{Option } C: (30\% +/- 4.1) = 25.9\% \text{ to } 34.1\%$$
$$\text{Option } D: (40\% +/- 4.4) = 35.6\% \text{ to } 44.4\%$$

This means there is a *significant difference* between these two options and it is fairly certain that *Option D is favoured over Option C*. The implications of confidence intervals and statistical probability are that simple frequencies from survey research can mask the true meaning of the data, and if the role of probability and confidence are not considered in data interpretation, then tourism development decisions may be taken which are not justified by the actual research findings.

SUMMARY

This chapter has described a number of recommended techniques which can be used by destinations to help monitor and evaluate the effects of a tourism development strategy. Monitoring is a vital component in understanding whether a tourism policy, plan and programme has been effective in achieving its development objectives. If carried out, monitoring and evaluation should help detect both contributing and distracting factors which have a bearing on the success of the strategy. If something is shown not to be working as planned, a different approach may be warranted and adjustments made.

Monitoring should not be a one-off action but consistent and ongoing if it is to be effective. It should take place throughout all phases of the tourism development process and be supplemented on a regular basis. However, this takes time, knowledge and skills which may not all be readily available in every destination. While destination communities are ultimately responsible for managing their own industry, local tourism committees sometimes find themselves more in the role of facilitator or catalyst in the development process, with outside help needed to provide extra technical assistance, advice and research expertise. With this in mind, Chapter 10 discusses as series of *do's* and *don'ts* to consider when seeking to hire the specialist services of a professional tourism consultant.

FURTHER READING *on Measuring Success*

Norcliffe, G.B. (1982) *Inferential Statistics for Geographers: an introduction*. London: Hutchinson & Co.

Oppenheim, A.N. (1966) *Questionnaire and Attitude Measurement*. London: Heinemann.

Ritchie, J.R.B. and Goeldner, C.R. (1987) *Travel, Tourism and Hospitality Research: a handbook for managers and researchers*. New York: John Wiley & Sons.

Tull, D.S. and Hawkins, D.I. (1993) *Marketing Research, Measurement and Method* (6th edition). London: Prentice-Hall.

Veal, A.J. (1997) *Research Methods for Leisure and Tourism: a practical guide* (2nd edition). London: Pitman Publishing.

World Tourism Organization (1996) *What Good Tourism Managers Need to Know*. Madrid: WTO.

CHAPTER TEN

Getting extra help
Making the most of professional consultants

INTRODUCTION

This book has been written to assist towns, cities and other small regions to get to grips with the basic process of preparing a tourism development strategy. However, due to any number of reasons, it may be necessary for a community to seek outside help in pursuing this aim. Getting extra help with tourism development can take many forms, most often depending on local circumstance. For the majority of communities looking at tourism seriously for the first time, or seeking to improve their current position, a number of sources are often readily available. This may come in the form of government grants, other types of financial aid, technical assistance, or practical expertise in planning, development and marketing.

Financial help is the most variable of all forms of assistance. Changing opportunities, priorities and policy means that getting financial aid from government and other 'public' or private sources is never constant, and hence not covered in detail in this chapter. Nonetheless, given the diverse nature of tourism and its relationship with many different aspects of a destination's social and natural environment, it is worth checking what kind of help may be available from various sources at any one point in time. Chapter 3 discussed a number of local groups which may be able to help. Beyond this, several other regional or national organizations and agencies may offer some form of assistance or guidance not only in terms of finance, but also support in kind through expertise in such areas as planning, marketing, management, regulation and control, points of law, public relations and market research (see Figure 10.1).

However, even when extra help is forthcoming, it may still be necessary to seek further specialist advice from a professional tourism consultant. A destination may already have a very good idea of what it wants to do, but equally it may benefit from a consultant's view of what is realistic or feasible. While 'in-house' staff may be fully competent in their tourism role, there may be occasions when particular skills are missing, where a second opinion is desirable, or where time constraints may mean the extra pair of hands will make the difference between development going ahead or not at all. Unlike the purchase of tangible goods, however, which can generally be touched or felt before a decision is made, hiring the specialist services of a consultant tends to require a much different approach. With this in mind, this chapter first looks briefly at tourism consulting in general and then sets out a number of key points to consider in the recruitment, selection and appointment of a consulting service.

National, Regional and State Agencies*
Linked with Tourism Development and Management

Tourism Commission/Board	Sport, Leisure and Recreation
Tourism Industry Association	Tertiary and Higher Education
National Heritage/Cultural Heritage	Native/Aboriginal Affairs
National Parks and Protected Areas	Fish and Wildlife Services
Agriculture and Land Management	Environmental Protection Agencies
Business Development/Commerce	Mines and Mineral Resources
Internal/National Affairs	Museums/Arts Council
Land-use Planning	Employment/Labour
Transportation	Forestry

Figure 10.1: National, Regional and State Agencies with Tourism Links
*No attempt is made to indicate specific titles of different agencies or departments due to the wide variety of groups involved – as such, this list is only indicative and not exhaustive.

TOURISM CONSULTING

In most countries, tourism development planning is no longer the preserve of a public sector profession, or simply limited to the relatively small number of multinational planning and management firms. Tourism consulting is a growing business, and since the 1980s it has expanded rapidly in response to industry demands. New specialist services continue to develop in response to market conditions and government policy. Consulting firms now range in both size and quality, from traditional large multinational management agencies, to the more recent individuals specializing in specific aspects of tourism, such as transport, rural development, marketing or interpretation. Recent emphasis on quality, value for money and sustainability have generated much interest in new products, technical design and development advice, master planning, market research, segmentation, interpretation and promotions, to name a few, all generating more work for consultants.

The tourism industry is changing and all change brings new opportunities. A consultant may be needed to solve a specific or unexpected problem, or be part of a more active initiative. While consultants may be useful for most aspects of development work, they should be hired because of their specific experience and expertise, and their ability to contribute something new to the development discussion. At its best, using consultants can be highly beneficial, giving access to new skills, alternative approaches and innovative ideas. At its worst it can be time-consuming, ineffective and costly – not only in terms of the direct expenditure, but also in lost opportunity. Clearly, a destination will be looking for added value from this activity, and the right consultant, in the right place, and at the right time, can bring that added value to the development process.

Getting the best out of a consultant must be the main aim for those who employ them. Selecting the right consultant for the job is a means to this end. However, choosing from the growing number of private sector and university-based consultants, the range of services on offer and the very wide range of qualifications, can make this a daunting task. Making the most of a consulting service depends to a large extent on having an efficient selection procedure and proper contractual arrangements. Consultants can only bring new skills, new approaches and new ideas to task – if the brief is right. Given the risks involved in employing the wrong consultants, or of the project not achieving its objectives, a number of steps can be taken to help maximize this opportunity. This chapter now sets out a number of key points to think about when seeking to buy-in technical expertise, from setting the brief to report presentation, highlighting a number of the Do's and Don'ts in the selection and briefing of professional tourism consultants.

Pre-briefing Stage

At the very beginning of the consulting process, the destination (client) must be very sure of what it wants to achieve when seeking to employ a consultant. Even at this preplanning stage there are a number of key issues to consider which will influence the successful outcome of a consulting project. Unfortunately, some clients do not have a clear idea of what it is they want the consultant to do, beyond perhaps preparing a tourism development strategy. Invariably, the brief that is prepared and sent out to tender which is vague, does not contain adequate information or fails to identify specific or realistic outputs, is a waste of both time and money. Therefore, before preparing the consultant's briefing document:

DO:

✓ **Do identify the potential costs and benefits of the project.**
Examine exactly why it is necessary to buy-in the consulting
service. While there may be a number of valid reasons, such as lack
of time or expertise of in-house staff, occasionally the rush or
urge to hire a consultant overlooks the potential of those already
employed. Sometimes consultants are hired more for 'political'
reasons than anything else.

✓ **Do clarify exactly what the project seeks to achieve.**
What are its goals and objectives? It is all too easy to be vague
about the project's aims, which may lead to a report which neither
responds to the initial problem, nor relates to the long-term
development objectives of the destination. If necessary, follow
the procedures described in Chapter 6 for setting objectives, but
in the context of preparing the project brief.

✓ **Do establish one person in-house who will act as the project
manager.** It is very important for clients to identify someone who
will be the key point of contact with the consultants throughout
the consulting process. This person should be in a position of
seniority which gives them the background knowledge and access
to information which may be requested by consultants. It is also
important for other in-house staff to be aware of the project and
the level of involvement which may be expected of them.

✓ **Do identify the budget available, including project management
costs of in-house personnel.** The cost of a consultant is not just
the direct contract fees, but also includes the cost of management
time from in-house personnel who will need to answer questions,
interview consultants, provide data, analyse, summarize and report
the results. Ignoring the role of in-house staff in this process can
prove very detrimental and costly.

Once these issues have been addressed, the destination should be in a better
position to begin to put the tender document (consultant's brief) together.

Setting the Brief

When the briefing document is ready to be prepared, there are a number
of different elements which must be included. A good brief sent to the

right consultant will generally lead to a satisfactory conclusion. Its most obvious feature is clarity. Clients must know what they want from the consultant, and that the brief sets out an issue or problem which is reasonable to solve within the time frame and funds available for the work:

DO:

✓ **Do state the key objectives of the project**. From the preparation stage the destination should have a clear idea of what the project is meant to address. Ideally a project should be limited to 3 or 4 key objectives, providing a central focus for the work. A study with several objectives will not produce a very coherent outcome, and the quality of work may suffer if consultants are expected to do too many things within a limited budget.

✓ **Do treat the brief as provisional**. It is important to retain some degree of flexibility in what is expected. Invariably, the tendering process will involve discussion with potential consultants who may suggest alternatives, which the client may have overlooked or discounted in error. Maintaining some degree of flexibility allows the client to take on board these new ideas, which tend to make for a better project.

✓ **Do state the expected outputs from the project**. The project brief should clearly state what it is the consultant is expected to produce. This does not mean the specific content, but rather the type of information to be included. If the project is meant to produce a final report, what this should contain must be clearly specified, such as description or analysis of the issues, policy recommendations, statistical data, recommendations on development options, or perhaps a detailed development strategy.

✓ **Do indicate the approximate budget for the project**. Consultants work for money and aim to earn a profit. They cannot sensibly plan the work without knowing what the level of remuneration is going to be. Setting a price range in advance also means they will be able to calculate the level of service they can provide, while putting the destination in a better position to compare submitted tenders in terms of quality and value for money. It is also important to set out the ground rules clearly from the start and decide whether the contract will be on a fixed fee plus expenses or on a lump-sum basis.

✓ **Do suggest a time frame for the project**. This should indicate when the project will commence, and include a time when the final report should be delivered (from commissioning), when interim reports will be required, if appropriate, and the number and timing of briefing sessions between the consultant and client steering group. This information is relevant to consultants so they can judge the timing of their work, know when key deadlines will appear in relation to their other workload, and determine whether or not they feel they can actually do the work. It is also very useful to include some indication of when interviews are likely to take place and when the project will be commissioned.

✓ **Do state conditions of copyright**. It is important to establish early on who will own the project documents, and what this means in terms of professional copyright, patents or intellectual property rights. Some consultants will want to retain copyright of the material they have produced, equally some clients will want to claim total ownership, after all they paid for the work. This point is particularly important where the consultants have been employed to produce ideas for specific facilities or attractions which the client would not want to see replicated, without significant variations, in another competing tourist destination.

✓ **Do specify what the tender should include**. In addition to stating project outcomes, maximum length for the proposal, how it should be organized and the delivery deadline, the briefing papers should also indicate what other information is required of the consultants when submitting tenders. This is likely to include details on:

♦ how the work will be carried out (methodology);
♦ the specific sources of information to be used (where appropriate); an indication of current terms and conditions of business (in confidence);
♦ detailed staff résumés of experience for those who will be undertaking the work, and an indication of their project role;
♦ the number of days to be spent on each aspect of the work, who will do this work, and the day rates being charged or applied;
♦ an overall timetable for the work including a Gantt chart (time line/flow chart) of the work schedule;
♦ plus any additional expenses which make up the project costs.

All of this information should be included in the tender submission, however, the smaller the project and its budget, the less detail should be required, otherwise it can make the whole tendering process commercially non-viable from the point of view of the consultant.

✓ **Do call a consultant for informal advice**. If in any doubt about these points, most consultants will be happy to discuss them informally over the phone, especially if it means they will be sent an invitation to tender later on. Most consultants will welcome the opportunity to discuss a client's needs, difficulties and time constraints if it leads to a well-thought-out brief. After all, an organized client with a clear idea of what they require makes the consultant's life much simpler and straightforward.

DON'T:

✗ **Don't overload the project brief with multiple objectives**. If there are too many points to be addressed, the overall quality of the work is likely to suffer. All projects have limits to what can be achieved within a specific time frame and budget. If there are several objectives to be considered, it may be more appropriate to prioritize these and where possible, leave some out, possibly to be taken up by some future consulting project. It is not always best practice to try to cover all issues at once, as this may lead to a sub-optimum solution.

✗ **Don't expect miracles with little money**. Project funding represents a key issue for consultants when responding to a brief. The scale of the problem to be resolved needs to correspond with the funds available. If the project brief seeks to answer more questions than the funds suggest, the client runs the very serious risk of paying for something which may be relatively worthless.

✗ **Don't be too rigid with what is expected**. While it is important to identify the context of what is needed, don't dictate what the report should conclude. This will undoubtedly lead to a report which fails to live up to its objectives. Being **too** rigid can undermine the ability of consultants to bring new or innovative ideas to the task. By all means discuss in-house ideas and expect these to be reviewed, but allow some flexibility as to their inclusion in the final analysis or list of options.

✗ **However, don't leave the brief too open**. This will likely draw a vague response, with no real solution offered. While it is important to allow consultants a certain degree of 'professional licence', if there is no real guidance or direction on current thinking by the client, the project outcome will most likely not move the issue forward, address real concerns of the destination, and will probably represent a significant waste of time and money.

Sending the Brief out to Tender

When the briefing papers are all prepared, the next stage is to draw up a list of consultants who will be sent the brief and be invited to respond. However, deciding on who to ask, or where to go to get this information can sometimes prove unwieldy:

DO:

✓ **Do put together a list of potential consultants**. Use source lists where they are available. Ask the national or regional tourist board for advice, and in some cases, maybe even ask them to tender for the work. Ask colleagues in other departments, other destinations, or other organizations for advice. It is also useful to discuss with these contacts, their experience in using different consultants to help give some idea as to their suitability and quality of work before deciding on their inclusion in the invitation to tender.

✓ **Do keep the tender list to 4 or 5**. This is a number taken seriously by most consultants. While some clients prefer to send out invitations to 10 or 12 consultants, this is really in no one's best interest. If all 12 submit proposals, that means 12 sets of documents to consider and review. This is not only very time-consuming, but also very difficult to give an adequate, equitable and fair comparison of the proposals. In addition, if consultants feel that their chances of success are small (which they clearly are with large tender lists) then they may actually decide not to submit a proposal. Keep the number of invitations in proportion to the scale of the proposed project.

✓ **Do allow adequate time to respond**. Consultants tend to be very busy people, and it is not in anyone's interest to send out a project brief and expect a detailed proposal by return. On average, clients should allow 3–4 weeks for the consultants to organize their team, develop their methodology, discuss points with the client and prepare their response. It is also best to avoid sending out briefing documents with 'end of year', 'new year' or 'tax year' submission dates. While these times tend to correspond with budget dates and the 'last-minute spending spree', they also tend to reflect bottlenecks in consulting work and may lead to a less than adequate submission.

✓ **Do designate a point of contact**. Ideally the client should have someone in-house, preferably the designated project manager, who will be able to answer questions, amend the brief and show consultants around if necessary. Project briefs and tender submissions are a means of communication, but no matter how well prepared, there will inevitably be some points that need further clarification or where different ideas emerge on how to best approach an issue. Good consultants will have a number of relevant ideas, and will want to discuss these with the client to ensure the proposal best fits the client's needs.

✓ **Do keep a record of consultants used for different projects**. It is very useful to keep a record of those asked to submit proposals and some indication of how well these all met the project specifications in the brief. If this list is kept up to date, it will help with future consulting projects and help establish a preference list of those more likely to respond favourably to future project opportunities.

DON'T:

✗ **Don't use the shotgun approach**. Ideally the tender list should be kept relatively small, with consultants selected on the basis of their expertise and direct relevance to the project under consideration. Long lists tend to reflect uncertainty in the client as to whom is better suited to undertake the work. It means more work for the client to liaise with potential consultants, to meet with them, to provide background information and to assess their proposals. If the project is multidisciplinary, it is best to target a lead consultant and let him put together the necessary expertise required for different aspects of the work.

✗ **Don't just use the same consultants as before**. While consultants used on a previous project may have delivered a very good report, and addressed all the issues, they may not always be suitable for the new project. The consultant may have developed a good working relationship with the destination and can be relied upon to produce quality work, but this may not always provide the optimum solution to the problems at hand. If the same consultant is used again and again, there will be nothing with which to compare their work. A fresh mind or an alternative approach may be worth considering and going out to tender is likely to produce this.

✗ **Don't demand an immediate detailed response**. While it is appropriate and good professional practice for consultants to acknowledge receipt of the brief and their likelihood of tendering for the work, do not ask for a detailed response straight away. If the project proposal is to be well constructed, the consultant will need some time to think it through. Busy, and generally good consultants will not be waiting around for the next brief to drop through their letter-box. Given adequate time, the vast majority of consultants will meet the tender deadline (although not necessarily the final report deadline).

Selecting the Best Proposal

Once proposals have been received from those four or five invited to tender for the project, it is now time to evaluate them against the brief and prepare a shortlist for interview. Shortlisting tenders should initially be done on the basis of how well they fulfil the brief set by the client. Other points to consider include the consultant's technical capability to carry out the work, aspects of quality assurance, estimated project costs, financial security of the firm, and where appropriate, professional indemnity:

DO:

✓ **Do match the proposed work against the brief**. On a scale of 1 to 10, assess the various components of each tender, including the proposed methods of work or analysis, consulting personnel and experience, and the suggested programme of work, in terms of how well these will deliver what is required. In addition:

♦ technical ability can play a significant role in matching consultant expertise with project issues – previous project experience, academic qualifications and professional membership are all points to consider;

♦ quality assurance procedures are also important – while certification such as ISO9000 is not absolute, some indication of quality systems should be indicated by the consultants;

♦ financial security of the firm and its ability to complete the work is another feature to consider, especially if the project is intended to take a long time to complete; and

♦ depending on the type of work being carried out, the ability of the consultants to offer professional indemnity insurance may be another necessary component of the tender analysis.

Once all points have been considered, add up the points awarded to each tender. This will give an initial rough indication of which proposals best fulfil the project specification.

✓ **Do choose three consultants as a shortlist to interview**. On the basis of the tender documents (and previous analysis), make a shortlist of those consultants who seem best able to deliver what is required. Rarely should a shortlist be more than four, as this would suggest the initial assessment of tenders was not critical enough. In contrast, a shortlist of two does not really allow for mistakes to be made in selecting the shortlist. Occasionally a written proposal may seem viable, but the interview may show this assessment as unwarranted. A shortlist of three gives some flexibility with the final decision, without being too time-consuming.

✓ **Do identify points for further clarification**. Invariably there may be a few points which are not absolutely clear in the tender, or which may be of particular interest and would benefit from an oral explanation to supplement the written text. These points can be discussed with the consultants when/if invited to interview, but be sure to inform those invited of the format which the interview process will take and the issues which need further discussion.

✓ **Do meet those shortlisted face to face**. Interviewing a shortlist of consultants serves a useful function for both the consultants and the client. The consultants are offered the chance to clarify any issues or gaps in the tender document, address client concerns and emphasize key points and strengths of their particular proposal. For the client, the interview offers the opportunity to hear firsthand what the consultant is proposing, and to investigate any aspect which seems unclear. If the project is complex, if there are certain elements which need better explanation, or if there are options to be considered, then it is vital that these details are sorted out at this stage. Many contracts are won or lost on the strength of the tender interview.

✓ **Do be clear about who is going to do the work.** Often consultant tenders will include senior personnel as lead consultants or project managers, however, in reality they may have very little to do with the actual project. This is common practice in consulting firms, and is used to make full use of a firm's resources. During the interview, be clear about who is going to be involved and at what level of participation, whether they attend the interview or not so as to avoid any misunderstandings later on. It is also important the person nominated as the consultant's project manager participates in the interview process, and agrees to inform the client of any new or additional staff brought in to undertake any of the work.

✓ **Do keep the interviews friendly.** The interview element in project selection is not only meant to clear up issues and to seek further clarification, but also to see how well the client and consultant will possibly work together. While it is important to maintain a professional relationship, projects tend to run much smoother when both the client and consultant have enough trust and professionalism to relax, work issues through together and perhaps discuss other things beyond the technical aspects of the project. A sense of humour is always useful, either as the client or consultant. If either the interviewers or interviewees appear antagonistic, defensive, patronizing or uninterested in the whole process, this will not likely lead to a very rewarding working relationship.

✓ **Do ensure the interview panel is well prepared.** Keep the interview panel to three to four well-informed members of the in-house project steering group or team. This should include the in-house project manager and two to three other people who have helped prepare the brief, have read the tenders in detail and can be relied upon to participate by asking intelligent questions. Ill-informed interviewers waste time and tend to make superficial decisions which can prove both costly and destructive to the development programme.

✓ **Do keep the interviews to a schedule**. Allow approximately 75 minutes for each interview cycle, as this gives plenty of scope for presentation, discussion, assessment and changeover. While it is unprofessional for the consultants to be late for the interview, it is equally unprofessional for clients to keep them waiting because a previous session seriously overran. The 75-minute cycle should help to avoid these problems, and with three interviewees, this should mean the whole process can be conducted in one afternoon.

✓ **Do choose the interview location carefully**. Most consultants will use some form of audio-visual equipment during their presentation. To make the most of this medium, the interview room should be big enough to allow the interview panel to see the projection screen unhindered, and where possible allow for a black-out of any unnecessary light source. Ask the consultants what equipment they may need to make their presentation before they arrive, so there aren't any last-minute scrambles to find an overhead projector or video playback facility.

✓ **Do ask for two or three examples of similar work**. As part of the interview process, it is legitimate for the client to ask consultants to give two or three examples of other work they have completed in a similar context in the recent past. Asking consultants to identify the issues, their response and outcome of the work is a useful means of comparative analysis. A good consultant with a record of delivering work on time, to budget and to specification will be pleased to refer potential clients (accepting confidentiality) to a previously satisfied customer. Recommendations are as important to the consultant as they are to the client and referrals are a key method of getting new business.

DON'T:

✗ **Don't decide purely on price**. Although financial pressures are a major concern, the best consultant for the job is not necessarily the one with the lowest tender price. The briefing document is a guide, and it is very likely that some consultants will submit a proposal which exceeds the target price. If the details of the bid warrant the extra costs, and this work meets the project specifications, the tender should not be rejected out of hand. If, however, the tender price exceeds the guide price by a considerable margin, then there should be cause for concern, especially if this has not been adequately explained in the proposal. Equally, cheaper projects may well reflect a poorly developed proposal, or 'minimalist' approach to the project, which in turn may lead to an unsatisfactory conclusion.

✗ **Don't interrogate the consultants**. The interview process is not meant to put consultants on the spot or trick them, but to offer further dialogue and explanation of the proposal. If the tender has made it to the shortlist, the clients should have a good idea of what it contains and what is proposed. Interrogation-style interviews tend to suggest a lack of awareness and preparedness on the part of the client, not major gaps or short-comings in the consultant's tender document. Equally, it is less than fair to ask consultants if they can modify the work, change their methods, add new things or cut their price in the middle of the interview. These may be valid points, but they cannot be fairly assessed in the context of an interview on either side of the discussion.

✗ **Don't be swayed simply by glossy or slick presentations**. It is very easy to get caught up in the technical aspects of project presentations. Glossy brochures, slick presentations and high-tech equipment give the impression of a well-produced proposal, but this does not necessarily mean the actual content of what is being offered is any better than the low-tech approach.

COMMISSIONING THE PROJECT

Once the interview process is complete, and the client has decided who will be awarded the project, it is time to prepare a contract and commission the work. Contracts do not need to be overlong, detailed or technical documents, because this will only delay the project start dates further with the editing and rewriting of contract documents. Generally, a simple letter of appointment, referring to the tender documents, will be sufficient:

DO:
✓ **Do set up a 'formal' contract with the consultant**. A simple standard contract should be drawn up which states what is to be done, when, by whom and when the results will be delivered and methods of payment. While this seems a lot, it can actually be done by a relatively simple letter which clearly identifies these points

and includes a copy of the consultant's proposal, along with any amendments agreed in writing between the two parties. The consultant should, upon receipt, confirm their acceptance of the project commission in writing.

✓ **Do set a project start date**. There will most likely be some delay between commissioning the project and work commencing. Most consultants will slot the work in as soon as possible once the appointment has been confirmed. However, if the original briefing papers requested information on likely start dates, plus a timetable for the tendering process, this delay should not be more than a couple of weeks. Set a timetable for the work, as discussed in the tender, but be prepared for the unexpected – work always changes in the consulting process. Retain a degree of flexibility.

✓ **Do inform unsuccessful bidders**. There are always losers in the tendering process, and these people should be informed as soon as possible of the client's decision. From the selection process it should be relatively obvious why one proposal was chosen over another. While most consultants would clearly rather win the contract, they will also appreciate being told the reasons why they were unsuccessful, including technical problems or personnel issues, project costs, or the presentation itself. This does not have to be in too much detail and most consultants will probably contest some of the reasons given. Invariably they will also like to know who has won the contract.

DON'T:
✗ **Don't award the contract at the interview**. While the interview panel may have a good idea of whom they would appoint immediately following the interview, it is best to record the reasoning and formally make the decision in the next day or two. This allows the panel a little time to collect their thoughts and not jump to any hasty conclusions which may prove unsatisfactory. After all it's not likely the consultants are going to start work on the project the following day. Don't keep interviewees waiting around for a decision on the day, but clearly state when the decision will be made and when they should expect to be informed of this.

Report Submission and Review

The last stage of the consulting process concerns the submission of the draft and final report, as well as a review of the consulting process from the client's perspective:

DO:

✓ **Do expect a draft edition of the consultant's report.** Before the final report is submitted, the consultants should prepare and submit a draft version of their ideas. This should contain a review of the problems and details of the proposed solutions. It should not be just a repetition of the briefing papers, nor simply restate in-house ideas with a little 'consultant's spin' to dress them up. The point of the draft report is to allow the clients to review the ideas, seek further clarification themselves, and suggest amendments which may make the final document more user-friendly, highlight key points or rework some ideas.

✓ **Do hold a debriefing session with the consultant.** It is generally useful to arrange a debriefing session with the consultant and the in-house team at the end of the contract. This can be used to assess the merits of the project, the conclusions and recommendations, discuss further opportunities, examine any stumbling-blocks and seek solutions to avoid future problems. Maintaining a good professional working relationship with clients is important to consultants, and most will seek to retain some level of contact with clients to ascertain when their services may be called upon again in the future.

✓ **Do hold an in-house debriefing session.** At the end of the project, it is also very useful for the in-house project team to be debriefed by the project manager. This should include a review of what worked well in the relationship with the consultant, was it money well spent, does the report really answer the questions, what might they do differently next time, what problems emerged, and how this could be overcome. It is also important to inform in-house staff what will happen next, and what if any aspects of the report's recommendations will likely be put into action.

DON'T:

✗ **Don't attempt to rewrite the draft report.** Submitting the draft report to the client is meant to provide them with the opportunity to comment on the proposals. It should not be used as an opportunity to change ideas, or seek to answer a new problem. However, it is valid to ask consultants to indicate other issues which have come to light, where further work may be required and how this might be addressed (of course they will probably do this anyway as a precursor to future contracts with the client).

FINAL POINT

Making the most of professional consultants often boils down to the experience and knowledge of individuals who readily apply the points discussed in this chapter. Some consulting projects seek specific solutions to poorly defined problems and this is often the root cause of many a poor project outcome. Good consultants value repeat work. They are well aware that this will only happen, however, where the projects they undertake are seen by their clients as meeting their needs, of high quality and completed on time. If destinations respond positively to the do's and don'ts discussed here then they should be much better placed to achieve a successful project outcome, within budget and on time.

Good luck!

REFERENCES

Blank, U. (1989) *The Community Tourism Industry Imperative: the necessity, the opportunities, its potential.* State College, PA: Venture Publishing.

Economist Intelligence Unit (1992) *The Tourism Industry and the Environment.* Special Report No. 2453, London: Business International Limited.

Edgell, D.L. (1990) *International Tourism Policy.* New York: Van Nostrand Reinhold.

Getz, D. (1991) *Festivals, Special Events and Tourism.* New York: Van Nostrand Reinhold.

Glasson, J., Godfrey, K. and Goodey, B. (1995) *Towards Visitor Impact Management.* Aldershot: UK, Avebury.

Gunn, C. (1988) *Tourism Planning* (2nd edition). New York: Taylor & Francis.

Gunn, C. (1994) *Tourism Planning: basics, concepts, cases* (3rd edition). Bristol, PA: Taylor & Francis.

Hughes, H.L. (1994), 'Tourism multiplier studies: a more judicious approach', *Tourism Management.* Vol. 15, No. 6, pp 403–406.

Kotler, P., Armstrong, G., Saunders, J. and Wang, V. (1999) *Principles of Marketing 2nd European Edition.* New Jersey: Prentice Hall.

Lane, B. (1989) *Will rural tourism succeed?* Conference on rural tourism development, Bristol University, December 1989.

McDonald, M. (1995) *Marketing plans. How to prepare them: how to use them* (3rd edition). Oxford: Butterworth-Heinemann.

Maister, D.A. (1985) 'The psychology of waiting lines', in Czepiel, J.A. *et al.* (eds) *The service encounter.* Lexington: Lexington Books, 113–123.

Mathieson, A. and Wall, G. (1982) *Tourism: economic, physical and social impacts.* London: Longmann Group UK Limited.

Middleton, V.T.C. (1988) *Marketing in travel and tourism.* Oxford: Butterworth-Heinemann.

Middleton, V.T.C. (1994a) *Marketing in travel and tourism* (2nd edition). Oxford: Butterworth-Heinemann.

Middleton, V.T.C. (1994b) 'The tourist product', in Witt, S.F. and Moutinho, L. (eds) *Tourism Marketing and Management Handbook* (2nd edition). Hemel Hempstead: Prentice Hall International.

Mill, R.C. and Morrison, A.M. (1985) *The Tourism System: an introductory text.* London: Prentice-Hall International.

Nelson, J. G., Butler, R. and Wall, G. (eds) (1993) *Tourism and Sustainable Development: monitoring, planning, managing.* Department of Geography Publications Series No. 37, University of Waterloo, Canada.

Norcliffe, J.G. (1982) *Inferential Statistics for Geographers: an introduction.* London: Hutchinson & Co.

Oppenheim, A.N. (1966) *Questionnaire and Attitude Measurement.* London: Heinemann.

Parasuraman, A., Zeithaml, V.A. and Berry, L.L. (1985) 'A conceptual model of service quality and the implication for future research'. *Journal of Marketing* (autumn), 141–150.

Parasuraman, A., Zeithaml, V.A. and Berry, L.L. (1988) 'SERVQUAL: a multiple-item scale for measuring consumer perceptions of service quality'. *Journal of Retailing,* 64 (spring), 12–40.

Poon, A. (1993) *Tourism, technology and competitive strategies.* Oxon: CAB International.

Ritchie, J.R.B. and Goeldner, C.R. (1987) *Travel, Tourism and Hospitality Research: a handbook for managers and researchers.* New York: John Wiley & Sons.

Ryan, C. (1991) *Recreational Tourism: a social science perspective.* London: Routledge.

Smith, S. (1989) *Tourism Analysis*. New York: Longmann Scientific & Technical.

Theobold, W. (ed) (1994) *Global Tourism: the next decade*. Oxford: Butterworth-Heinemann.

Tull, D.S. and Hawkins, D.I. (1993) *Marketing research. Measurement and method* (6th edition). London: Prentice-Hall.

Veal, A.J. (1997) *Research Methods for Leisure and Tourism: a practical guide*, (2nd edition). London: Pitman Publishing.

World Tourism Organization (1991) *Tourism to the year 2000. Qualitative aspects affecting global growth*. Madrid: World Tourism Organization.

World Tourism Organization (1996) *What good tourism managers need to know*. Madrid: WTO.

World Tourism Organization (1997a) *Shining in the media spotlight*. Madrid: WTO.

World Tourism Organization (1997b) *Tourism 2020 vision executive summary*. Madrid: WTO.

World Tourism Organization (1998) *Travel and Tourism Fairs*. Madrid: WTO.

Zeithaml, V.A. and Bitner, M.J. (1996) *Services marketing*. London: McGraw-Hill.

INDEX